First Quarter

For my siblings, my sons, my Sheila.

John Tuomey
First Quarter

THE LILLIPUT PRESS
DUBLIN

First published 2023 by
THE LILLIPUT PRESS
62–63 Sitric Road, Arbour Hill
Dublin 7, Ireland
www.lilliputpress.ie

ISBN 9781843518747

A CIP record for this title is available from The British Library.

10 9 8 7 6 5 4 3 2 1

The Lilliput Press gratefully acknowledges the financial support of the Arts Council/An Chomhairle Ealaíon.

Set in 11pt on 15pt with Adobe Caslon Pro by Compuscript
Printed in the Czech Republic by Finidr

Contents

Every generation goes its own way
and remembers only those things it wants to remember.
Roy Jacobsen, *The Unseen*

Preface

At it again, with your I's and me's!
Stendhal, *The Life of Henry Brulard*

I HAVE NO BACKGROUND in architecture, apart from my father's building sites. Both my parents came from well-established, solidly middle-class shopkeeping stock. And yet I feel that my identity, the first and last thing to say about me, is that I am an architect. Become one, not born one, but an architect through to the bone.

How did this happen? Simple to say. I went to university when I was seventeen years old to find myself transported, suddenly, into my natural world, a life-world that was waiting. I knew right away.

My mother, at nineteen, had slipped away from her Limerick business upbringing, dodging the prospect of joining her father, Jack Walsh, in his fire-lit office at Cannock's department store, where three of his daughters went to work, where he had followed his father. She left home to take up a job in the bank, moving digs all around the country town circuit, feeling independent and fancy free, until she fell in with my father at a tennis party in Tralee. She brought me up, from my earliest days, with the idea instilled of self-reliance. Moving on, moving out.

A new life in architecture lay ahead of me. Everything before was behind me. Time to move on, I said to myself, with never a backward glance. Until now. Not so simple, after all. Here I am, trying to piece together a mosaic of places and a partial history of events, trying to recall what it was that might have made me what I am. Now, well past the midway point, to remember before I forget. Where I came from. How I found my way from there to here. Not to here exactly, but up to the starting point that brought me here. Here I am.

Ten Years' Time

It is not the literal past, the 'facts' of history, that shape
us, but images of the past embodied in language.

Brian Friel, *Translations*

I DON'T REMEMBER, CAN'T remember, the house where I was
born. Not that I was born in a house. I was born in a hurry
at the Bon Secours in Tralee. My mother didn't have time to
remove her sheepskin boots, or so the story goes. The little
house I was brought back to faced Fenit's main street. Folded
in under the roof was a veranda; this is known to me only
from one tiny black-and-white photograph, with my father,
ever the gardener, ministering to, admiring perhaps, a very
large cabbage. He'd been working for more than two years
as site engineer for the new Fenit pier, an elongated isthmus
leading to Europe's most westerly deep-sea harbour, not five
miles from his family home at the Spa. I don't know, and
it's too late to ask him now, why he took this, his first job, so
close to his original home place, when he'd been so far away
all through the war. The new family, my mother, father and
firstborn sister, lived on a daily diet of lobster, my father being
known locally as 'Lobster King Tuomey' for his luck with the
pots. Spartan luxury.

Then there was Macroom, where we moved when
I was six months old, my father this time working on a

town water scheme. We lived in a plain-fronted terraced house on Main Street. There was a long back garden, a narrow strip between high walls, where he grew vegetables. I have a dim, or dimly received, memory of very large marrows

Images begin to take shape, still hazy but a little clearer, from our days in Drumshanbo, where we once again rented a terraced house on the main street. Here my father was stationed to build new structures for the coal mines at Arigna, an electricity-generating power plant built to burn the locally mined fuel. One day he brought me inside a very tall chimney, looking up together through the tapering shaft to a little slot of sky, him telling me about the constellations, so it must have been evening time. The Plough pointing to the Pole Star, the Seven Sisters in a huddle, Cassiopeia like a big W, Sirius the Dog Star, the brightest star in the sky. These lessons in basic astronomy continued across camping holidays and from the kitchen step on summer nights.

I began my schooldays in Drumshanbo. The schoolmaster, in a gesture of welcome, showed me how to milk his cow. Warm air inside the dark cowshed, warm milk in a bright bucket. Another day, on the way home from a shopping trip to Carrick-on-Shannon, I threw my new shoes out of the car window, silently, one at a time, each at some distance from the other along the country road, this careful tactic adding, I've been told, to my parents' frustration. My older sister's back seat of the car frustration lay in trying to teach me words, with instructions to repeat after her … Cow, *Cow*. Horse, *Horse*. House, *Outhouse*. I don't know why it infuriated her so, my insistence on outhouse, but then again, I've been told, it worked time after time. Still, it's a nice word, outhouse. Sometimes you can make yourself believe you've invented or discovered even the simplest of words, a sudden moment of epiphany. I remember wasting time as a student thinking about the etymology of the word *diagram*, the diagrammatic clarity of the word itself, already marked out in lines.

There was some sort of arrangement with the landlord that, on market days, he could pen his sheep in the hall of our house, lining the floor and halfway up the walls with corrugated sheeting. We looked out of the front window at wall-to-wall sheep, sheep spread across and up and down the street. Could this be true? At the back was another high-walled long garden where my sister and I climbed along its stone ledge, made snowmen with tin hats and coal buttons and, again, my father grew his vegetables. Visions of the Virgin and Child appeared over the wall, blurred and radiant figures shimmering in our neighbour's round-arched landing window, worrying me: what was *She* trying to tell me? After my mother took me to get my first pair of glasses, those disconcerting visions disappeared for good. Sliding down the stairs on a tray and shunting the tray-train into its station under the kitchen table, my own private station for ego-stretching and pestering exchanges with my ever-attentive mother. Who would I be, where would I be, without the sense of purpose driven deep by my mother? She came home from Sligo with the new baby, my middle sister, who still believes she belongs in the west. So now, on the long drive back down south, we were three in the back of the car.

That long drive was to Cobh, where my father's company had the contract to build new ground for the Haulbowline Island steelworks. From Kerry to Cork, to Leitrim and back to Cork, four house moves through three counties by the time I was five. In these place-based recollections of childhood, memories from Cobh come more strongly into focus and are more likely to be first hand, their reliability tempered only by the normal distortion of six decades' distance. If they are not really all true, they are all certainly real. Our street-fronting flat led back to a tiny yard where a red sandstone rockface ran weeping with water. No room for vegetable growing here. I slept on an iron frame bed in a side pocket off the hallway, a bed-sized alcove in the undercroft of the stairs to the upstairs flat. I lay defended by a wooden sword laid across my chest, made for me by my father, bluntly pointed at its white-painted tip, sanded off on its second day to a safer chamfer, its hilt painted silver and gold. I was not scared in the dark, not until the night when, brushing my teeth in the bathroom at the end of the hall, I glimpsed in the mirror a hooded figure loping out of the gloom. I turned round to see this creature bounding up behind me, long arms swinging low to the floor. My heart jumped. The bogeyman leapt sideways into the shadow. Out stepped my laughing father, his human face half-hidden by a monkey mask, removing the disguise of his oversized duffel coat. His joke, not so funny for me.

Our first Cobh Christmas delivered a handmade red-painted wooden train, steam engine and carriage, solid enough to sit astride and ride around the flat, but not for the outdoors, the street being too steep to go railing. Harbour Hill is a really steep street, running down and around a dogleg bend to the small harbour at the centre of town, where my father kept a shiny varnished sailing dinghy, *Shearwater II* – was there ever a first to this second? It was our only boat, and leaving it behind when we moved again was a blow to the heart. One day, I noticed a carton of golf balls in the bottom of the boat. One by one, I dropped them in the water, announcing, with the empty box held out as evidence of a successful experiment, 'Daddy, I've news for you. Golf balls don't float!' No ice cream that day.

The day of the ice cream was when I tripped over a stray rope while trying to pull the dinghy up the slip. I was picked up crying, with scraped hands and knees, a bloodied nose, a sore and swollen upper lip, by my aunt, my mother's younger sister, who was staying with us at the time. She brought me into a little timber-boarded sweet shop across the road from the pier and bought an eight-penny wafer, the biggest I'd ever seen, intended, I now suppose, to reduce the swelling. Opened up out of their boldly striped red and white packaging, those blocks of vanilla ice cream would have been carefully marked out in scored lines ready for dividing. Shopkeepers had a special trowel-like gadget for doing this, three-penny slices being the usual measure on a Sunday after mass. I'd broken my front tooth in the fall, so that extra thick treat brought more nerve pain than pleasure that day, but a memorable pleasure nonetheless. Another day we sailed all the way around the sheer-sided hull of the two-funnelled *Mauretania* as she was towed into harbour. We bobbed with excitement in her wake. Years later, in London, watching Fellini's *Amarcord*, with all the awestruck townspeople out in their boats, waiting in silent rapture for a passing liner's emergence out of the dark, brought me sailing back to Cobh.

That patient aunt, on this or another visit, was to reveal a particular flaw in my character, a persistent flaw, one not to be proud of. Pride. Noticing my interest in her knitting patterns, she sat down beside me, with needles and wool, and gently offered to show me how to knit. I stood up and made my escape, declaring over my shoulder, 'I can knit!' This moped-pedalling aunt was an unusual woman, independent living, chain smoking. She enrolled me for an annual subscription to *Animals* magazine, with its own embossed and rigid folder to bind all the weekly issues in neat order. She always arrived with interesting books: *The Social Life of Animals*, by Marcel Sire, with its description of forty thousand bees working together in a hive, made a lasting impression.

She drove up from Limerick to mind us five children when I was twelve, a few years after the family had moved to Dundalk, while my parents went off on their first non-family holiday, two weeks in Venice. On the first day we clashed over boundaries, she being too strict, or maybe too careful, never having looked after a houseful of children, me demanding to spend the long summer days unstructured by any aunt-imposed lunch or dinner schedules. I hot-headed for the door and cycled off to the Blackrock baths for a cooling swim. That same day my bicycle was stolen from outside the swimming pool. I tramped the four-mile journey home, lamenting that surely my hard-won freedom would be severely curtailed. My aunt promptly placed an ad in the local newspaper, simply asking for information leading to the bicycle's return. The next day, I received a mysterious letter from an unnamed Redemptorist, asking me to call to the monastery if I wished to learn something to my advantage. I turned up at the appointed hour, cryptic letter in hand, and was surprised to be led to a dark shed full of discarded bicycles. Bicycles by the dozen, I was told, dumped daily over the monastery wall by boys spinning home from the pool, ditching their borrowed wheels as they crossed the railway bridge back into town. I could pick any bike, but my own shiny Raleigh was ready and waiting. Independence was re-established, and relations with my aunt much improved.

Years later, while my mother was minding her ailing sister, I volunteered to investigate how to fulfil her last wish. I made an appointment at the Royal College of Surgeons, just a short walk from our Dublin studio in Camden Row. I was ushered to a small office upstairs, where a woman welcomed me, invited me to sit down and tell her what was on my mind. I explained that there was this aunt, who now lay dying in a Limerick hospital, how she had worked for doctors in her youth and always took an interest in science, and now she wanted to donate her body to medical science, not that I knew her very well, just wanted to help, none of the family was familiar with the procedure and I was here for any useful advice on what needed to be done. The kindly faced woman softly shut the door to the corridor, turned towards me with sympathy and compassion in her eyes, shaking her head slowly. 'There is no aunt in Limerick, is there? It's yourself, isn't it, it's you are the one who's dying. Why don't you tell me all about it?' I was stunned into silence by this strange experience. Once again, as often seemed to happen around this particular aunt, I stood up and made my escape.

My aunt's remains eventually landed in the pathology lab at University College Cork, the old anatomy building we have since redesigned and adapted to livelier purposes as a student hub. And a year or two after her deposition, I arranged the transfer of her coffin to Rocky Island, a crematorium most cleverly converted from the magazine fort, entered through tunnels cut out of the rock, a quiet place with beautiful vaulted brickwork and a sense of calm isolation, a feeling of final destination enhanced by the way it stands open to the water's edge. And so, in the end, at her end, I returned with my adventuring aunt to the wide bay of Cork Harbour, where we had sailed together when I was six.

Seen from the sea, from where it must surely have been designed to be seen, Cobh is tightly spread against the hillside, terraces stacked over each other, the vertical line of the four-stage cathedral spire keeping the whole pile-up pinned in place. Harbour Hill leads down in the direction of the Holy Ground, where the rough boys were rumoured to gather. From our doorstep, I witnessed a running group of lads with a rope stretched loosely between them from either footpath. A flick of the rope was enough to lasso passing girls, one after another, all looped together and trotting down the centre of the street in their summer dresses, the way the cowboys rustled wild ponies on the plains.

Coming home from school, in the shadow of the vast cathedral where I made my first holy communion, at the foot of the steps under its railinged walls, I was a few times set upon by a small gang closer to my own age. They wanted either my banana sandwich or my cardboard crown. They swung me to the ground by the second coat worn buttoned at the neck over my real coat, a flying cape to match my crown. I came home intimidated by what looked likely to become a pattern of low-level bullying. Indignant, dragging me with him, my father leapt into the car. He drove down the hill in pursuit, pulled up across the pavement, stepping out into the path of this little hooligan troupe to promise, in words I'd never heard him say, his hand raised like a hatchet, that he would split them from head to toe. No more trouble after this warning, not from that quarter.

One fine day I fell off a beach-facing cliff. An overhanging tuft of grass gave way and I dropped down some twelve feet to land, luckily, on a small patch of sand between jagged rocks. Broke my ankle in two places – 'That fellow will always land on his feet,' said my father to my worried mother. I learned to adopt a loping trot, like Long John Silver, hopping up and down Harbour Hill, one leg up on the padded knee-rest of my wooden crutch. The day my foot was released from its plaster cast, my father broke the crutch over his knee and burnt it in the fire. I felt bereft, deprived of the advantage of my pirate's prop.

Two doors up the street lived my first love, who one day needed to be rescued from the railings where the postman had her loosely tied by her long skinny plaits. The postman was known for such tricks, but this one gave me the chance to be useful. We used to dress up in brown paper vestments, she and my sister and I, taking it in turns to say mass, or concelebrate high mass together, arrayed side by side on the steps of her hallway. Her ancient aunt stood every day like a statue in the kitchen with her skirt pulled up, warming her backside against the range. The day of her auntie's death, that bold and lively girl led me upstairs through a house crowded with black-suited mourners, to feel with my fingers the stone cold of a dead woman's forehead.

In my father's typical style, with no explanatory words, he showed me how to ride my new red bicycle. Sat up on the saddle, feet set on the pedals, released at the top of a steep country lane, gaining speed in gathering panic, until, hands sweating, halfway down the gravelly hill, I pulled the front brake and turned over into the ditch. A scary start, sure enough, but I've never been without a bike since. I seem to think more clearly, believe myself in better balance of mind and body, when I'm up on a bike. Models come and go, dropped handlebars and racing frames are probably gone for good, but being in possession of a bicycle remains a pivotal part of my sense of identity.

Years later, teenage driving lessons with my father followed a similar pattern – finding out how to fend for yourself. He drove out one Sunday afternoon to a disused industrial estate. We swapped seats for a short demonstration of brake and accelerator with the right foot, clutch with the left. Then he stepped out of the car, leaving me at the wheel with only minimal instruction on gearstick manipulation. I can see him still, standing on the concrete road, smoking his pipe, watching calmly while I reversed his car right off the road and revved up onto a gravel mound. Lessons learned from my father, man of few words.

Four of us now, crammed into the back seat of the new Simca, all the way from Cobh to Cooley. My brother still laments having been translated out of his native county of Cork. Everything changes from black and white to colour with our move to Cooley, the crucible of my boyhood self-reliance. These days, that change in tone still happens, but now in reverse, since the field pattern of the Cooley Peninsula feels older than the ages, the rural landscape seems to belong in black and white. But in those crucial days, the whole scene shifted into Technicolor, coinciding with the dawn of my consciousness, the beginning of life as an individual. Or maybe that realisation only sank in on the upstairs balcony at the Carlingford cinema, Spartacus climbing over the railings of his captivity and *The Magnificent Seven* with its magnificent theme music. Many movies since have made lasting impressions, but these were the instigators.

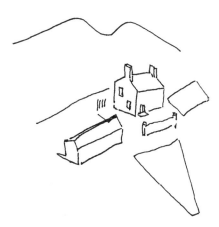

We settled into a plain and ordinary two-storey farmhouse, no farmland with it now, still a proper country house with walls and gate piers, red corrugated sheds and whitewashed outhouses, iron gates and compartmentalised gardens ready for my father to plant his vegetables. We kept chickens, ducks, rabbits, many cats, the occasional hedgehog held overnight under a galvanised bucket. On its road side, Hillview looked over a low mountainy prospect up to Maeve's Gap, ready every morning for the Gaelic queen to ride out of the mist into a new cattle raid. The outriding walls were integral to the house, indivisible from the main structure, long walls leading to promontory gate piers, bastions of outlook to nearby fields and faraway hills. Straddling the wall outside the back door, with two breakfast cereal boxes strung behind for saddlebags, the gate pier was your horse's head, straining for the open country. Standing on the furthest pier, you were a pirate's boy sent to the crow's nest to keep a weather eye on the horizon for passing ships. Behind the pebbledash boundary walls, the house was surrounded by a time-woven tapestry of odd-sized fields, each one soon named: the Green Field, the Big Field, the Far Field. Over the rise beyond these differently shaped plots were big patches of brambles, tangled underworlds, one with a drystone sweathouse, tiny, overgrown, earthen-floored, but spacious enough to crawl into and waste away the day. And beyond that, too far to walk to but not too far to wonder about, lay the sea, the sloping sandy beach and the eastern horizon. On a clear day you could see the Isle of Man from the nearest hill.

The house itself a simple double-fronted block with brick chimneys on the gables. Central narrow hall, single-flight stair. My room upstairs, roadside, on the north-west corner, watching Maeve's Gap. The front garden, seen from above, lay in two lawns divided by a narrow concrete path from a red-painted gate, never used, leading to a snout-projecting porch and front door, likewise never used. Upstairs I set traps for my sister, standing on a chair to place soaking wet sponges strategically balanced over her half-open bedroom door, her door across the hall from mine. Once I threw her teddy down the hall from the top of the stairs. She ducked, the teddy smashed through the window, just as the farmer from down the road, known only as Mr Mac, was cycling by, coming in to see how we were, my parents being out. He diplomatically cleared the broken glass off the porch roof and courteously retrieved my sister's teddy. Not all my fault, he agreed. My aim was good, my sister's fault for ducking.

Any callers came in the big gate at the side of the house, across the main yard, through the small gate to the back yard, up two steps to arrive, unannounced or uninvited, straight in the back-kitchen door. A pulley drying rack hung from the kitchen ceiling, over the Rayburn range. The main clothesline ran across the yard, squares of laundry useful for bow-and-arrow target practice, until my sister appeared from behind a flapping tea towel with a floating arrow caught in her cheek, just below the eye. Target practice moved on to duck eggs lined up along the top of the wall, a more demanding job and best tackled with a catapult. My weekly housework, apart from mealtime washing up with my sister – you wash, I'll dry – was to hoover the hall and stairs, polish the brass knocker of the unused front door, polish the bent parallel lines of copper pipework in the bathroom, polish the family shoes ready for Sunday mass. My father made the sandwiches for our school lunches and for his own lunch at work, cooked the chicken for Sunday lunch and the turkey for Christmas dinner. Otherwise, assuming my sisters did no work – they had no regular duties that I can recall – my lively mother ran the house. I ran all around that house with my mother, chased her for sport, until the day of her fortieth birthday, when shocked by her age, I decided she was too old for dashing about after her boy.

It wasn't too far to walk to school, maybe another mile beyond Maguire's Cross, but some days needed an early start.

Each week, one boy was selected, given the honour, to come in half an hour before school to set and light the stove. It was a two-storey schoolhouse, standing foursquare in the shadow of a disused railway bridge over the road to Grange. Our classroom was on the first floor, accessed by an outside stair, one of two rooms subdivided by a glazed partition. There were a few rituals worth recording here.

The first offender of the week would be asked to go out along the roadside, entrusted with the teacher's penknife, to cut a sally stick from the hedgerow for his own punishment and, inevitably, for others' punishment to follow. Too small a stick and the teacher would go out and choose his own, too heavy and everybody suffered, so, by an unspoken understanding, every stick got cut to something like a standard size. Except once, as I recall, when some joker brought back a long and wavy sapling, thinking it too unwieldy to be useful. It turned out to be the worst week for stinging smacks. That springy stick, flicked like a whip from the teacher's station, could reach any ear on any desk at random. Our desks were long benches, four to a row, with sunken inkwells filled daily, blue ink carefully poured out from a big bottle of Quink, another privilege designated weekly.

A central spine wall divided the schoolyard between boys and girls, with the toilets in a lean-to shed built against the back wall, just under the railway line. A continuous wooden seat ran between stalls, with circular cutouts over an open drain. That drain, by gravity's natural fall, joined the boys' yard through to the girls'. A small flat stone, pegged at the correct angle through one of the holes in the bench, could be aimed to skip along the drain and, on a good day, splash up the innocent backside of an unseen target. In this game of chance, calm and unidentifiable, you simply waited for the scream.

Lodged in my school experience, after a short introductory stint in Drumshanbo, two years in Cobh and two more in Cooley, is the estranged feeling of speaking with a different accent from whatever boy sat beside me in school. I must have started out with a Cork sing-song, flattened off in Leitrim, tuned up again in Cobh and further confused by the time we got to Cooley. It stays with me, this sense of separation, a mild unease in social situations, unsettled, not fully belonging in the room.

Midway through second class, pupils and teachers gathered to witness the old schoolhouse being closed up in preparation for demolition, then set off in a festive parade half a mile down the country road to the new building, one of the ubiquitous high-windowed, steep-roofed 1960s national schools, surrounded by low walls, entered via a wedge-shaped stile, pebbledash walls painted yellow ochre, with a water tower and flat-roofed stoa-like shelter between yard and playing field. There was a special sense of satisfaction, shared by all that day, the feeling of walking away from the old world, heading off to start anew.

We lived in the Bush, where the local shop was Savage's. Savages in the Bush; somehow these names stick in the mind. It sounds dangerous now, but I don't remember it being talked about as strange. On the way down to Savage's, just before the disused redbrick railway station, I would pass women gathered at the green-painted pump. With a bucket held in place by a bump on the spout, they pushed the creaky leaky curved handle up and down while they talked. I took it to be what it was, an everyday social occasion, but I missed completely what it meant – they didn't have running water in their houses. Unlike us, they weren't 'on the mains'. Carrying water was women's work, a good part of their day gone this way, back and forth with buckets. Sailing by on my red bike, back from the shop with gingernut biscuits, catching snippets of local chat, I was oblivious to the gender politics of the parish pump.

Bread was delivered twice a week; we ran out on the road to collect our batch loaf from the fragrant sliding shelves of the baker's van. The breadman brought us a cat, marmalade striped, christened Marmaduke, the chieftain of the many cats in that house. My mother made brown soda bread and raisin scones. Mr Mac cycled up every morning with a bucketful of milk swinging from his handlebars and hung that heavy bucket on our gate. He had a white horse called Prince, on whose wide back I was allowed to ride, and a black dog, also called Prince, that nobody was allowed to go near. The year we arrived, Prince the horse pulled the plough up and down the big field, first for potato planting and later for potato picking. We walked behind the horse-drawn plough, lifting potatoes, proud members of the meitheal. The second year, Mr Mac's new tractor drove the reaping and threshing in the Big Field, now renamed the Corn Field, and we tried to help with the haystacks, but mostly played with pitchforks. Mr and Mrs Mac walked up to our house to witness the arrival of the new television. Then, a few days later, they arrived with a sister, aunt of a famous Kilkenny goalie, Ollie Walsh, to watch the hurling final, all shouting at the television – 'Come on, Ollie!'

Television introduced masculine-coded subliminal influences via multiple weekly westerns. *Cheyenne*, whose book cover portrait I polished to a lustrous shine. The *Cheyenne Television Story Book 1961* was one of my first pocket money purchases. The spin-off *Bronco Layne*, politely muttering 'Much obliged, ma'am' in almost every episode. *The Lone Ranger*, likewise politely removing his hat, but never his mask, while he perched backwards on a swiftly swivelled chair. I soon affected this style of sitting, arms folded over the back of a kitchen chair. *Rawhide*, memorable mainly for all the wild hollering at cattle. *Champion the Wonder Horse*, the wild stallion streaking through box canyon hillsides to greet the only boy he could rely on. I was that boy. *Bonanza*, with the slow and burly Hoss Cartwright always on the lookout for his brother Little Joe. The three main men of *Bat Masterson*, *Maverick* and *Have Gun – Will Travel*, suave, dapper and besuited in black, were a little too smooth for me. So many cowboys drifting in on different evenings across British, Ulster and Irish television. Multi-channel choice was one advantage of this newly settled life below the border.

My father brought home a borrowed record player. It looked like a two-tone suitcase, red lid and beige body, leatherette handle, snap-fastened with brassy buckles. All the lights turned off, eyes closed in the dark, we sat by the fire listening to the 'Moonlight Sonata'. Was it this killed off the rosary? No more kneeling on the living room carpet, face down into the circled armchairs, for the nightly recitation of the mysteries. Sorrowful, Joyful, Glorious, all gone. The gloomy ritual replaced by the pleasure of listening to records. Along with the loan of the player came a set of 45rpm singles: 'Johnny Will', 'Tell Laura I Love Her', 'Just Tell Her Jim Said Hello'. I know every word of those songs. Upstairs in the box room, now become my father's art studio, probably left behind by a previous tenant, was a cardboard box of 78rpm records. Large in diameter and heavy in the hand, perfectly balanced for discus throwing. There was something satisfactory about gliding those shellac discs across the yard, watching them sail in a smoothly curved sweep under the clothesline until they smashed in shards against the pebbledash wall. A whole box of music destroyed in a morning.

Down at Maguire's Cross, they had a long pig that could be led to the top of the field and didn't seem to mind being ridden back down into the farmyard. You had to hold tight to his bristly ears to avoid being shaken off into the nettles. The farmer next door, a man named White, had an old goat, nameless, but tame enough to ride. The stink of goat is hard to lose. One night, in the middle of the night, that neighbour farmer rapped urgently on my parents' downstairs bedroom window, enlisting my father on the hunt for a badger. He was advised to put clinkers from the fire grate down inside his Wellington boots, so the badger, if he bit, when he bit, would hear the sound of breaking bone and release his grip. The poor badger was killed by a smack on the snout with the flat of a spade. My father didn't enjoy the outing, but he must have thought something of his unease could be assuaged by skinning the carcass. The badger skin hung stretched out to dry in the shed for a long time afterwards, its five extremities, four feet and a nose, pinned onto a wooden frame. Gruesome work for little useful gain. A more cheerful moment, in that same shed, was the delivery of a cardboard box of day-old chicks, quite the crowd, little yellow balls of fluff cheeping under the warmth of an infra-red lamp swinging from the rafters.

One summer's day a big box was brought from the building site, cross-roped and tied onto a flat back truck. An empty wooden crate, ten feet square, it must have been a container for a large piece of machinery. And, arriving with it, a big-bellied wooden barrel. These were hauled out into the middle of the Green Field. We learned to walk the barrel, balancing over the bumpy ground, wobbling up and down the field. The box had multiple applications. First, turned over on its side, as a theatre. The lid flapped down flat to make a stage platform. Inside the box a curtain was strung up to mark the upstage line between dressing and performance. You could climb up the back of the ledge-braced box to appear on top, adding a vertical dimension to the drama. Then, when the play ran out its season, when the parents had seen the show twice or three times, after the hoops fell off the barrel, the box became the wheelhouse for a cargo ship, with its shipshape outlined in barrel sections, curved boards aligned on the sea-green grass.

There were two ways into the Green Field. Ceremonially, occasionally, with the iron gate swung open, this only to bring something in or out, a box or a barrel, or for the regal arrival of an invited audience of parents and baby sister. For more everyday access, ordinarily, simply climb over the flat bars of the gate, step onto the waiting barrel, walk the barrel on a round-the-world voyage to bump up against the island cliffside of the box and alight safely on dry land. Brother and sisters enlisted as crew, steering a convoy across the choppy seas of the Green Field.

My father was not there when one of our hens fell suddenly ill. My mother insisted it must be dealt with immediately, a matter of urgency to safeguard the flock. I was sent out to deal with the sick hen. I knew that a hen could be killed, but not how. I'd helped to pluck chickens on Saturday nights for Sunday dinner, but I was new to the killing act. I took a sharp spade from the shed, set the wretched hen on a concrete block and hit a few clumsy blows to the neck. Using the same spade, after the death throes, I dug a shallow grave, deep enough to cover the corpse, keeping the sod intact to ensure an invisible interment, out of sight, out of mind. At last, the job finished, in a final flourish to rid myself of the guilt, I stamped with both feet on the burial site. A terrible squeal of a squawk came screeching out of the grassy ground. Had I buried the cursed creature alive? I ran like a hare to escape the wrath of the undead hen. It took time to convince me the chicken was not coming to get me, that what I had heard was only the explosive reflex caused by jumping on air-filled lungs. Far from comforted, I knew I'd been truly exposed as a townie, a pretender, not fit to survive in the country, never cut out to be a countryman to the core.

I was considered bright in that school in Cooley, encouraged by my teacher Mrs O'Connor, a motivating figure in my early education, to improve my mind by reading, for instance, the new weekly *Look and Learn*. The old church at Grange was the nerve centre of the dispersed rural settlement, its whitewashed architecture unchanged and old ways strictly observed, men on one side, women on the other, young families upstairs. Older men half-knelt in the porch, half-in half-out of the church, the genuflecting knee cushioned in the comfort of a cap dropped quietly on the cold floor. Slipping down fast from the balcony after mass, ducking between the legs of the adults, I could get to the shop to nab the Sunday papers and weekly comics ahead of all the slowcoaches. Reading was supplemented by Mrs Mac lending me her grown-up son's old cowboy stories, pocket-sized paperbacks printed on yellow-edged pulp paper, tales of the Wild West.

My youngest sister's only memory of Cooley is our leaving it behind, looking out at the removal van in the rain. Now there were five in the back of the car for the short drive to what would become the permanent family home in Dundalk. Or, to be more accurate, four of us in the back and one in the front, since we had bench seats back and front in those days. But, for me, looking back, Cooley was a place apart, a homeplace from our wanderings, and this sense of nostalgia set in early. If Dundalk was the destination my parents had settled on, with five children after six moves in ten years, I couldn't help wondering what's next, where to next?

The year before that final move, it was decided to send me into town to prep school at St Mary's College, a fee-paying school, known as the Marist, where I managed another few studious years of winning class prizes, dutifully adapting to altar boy training, lighting candles, carrying cruets, learning the Latin responses and mastering the patterns of ringing the bells, three times for the Sanctus, five for the various elevations around the consecration, the bells that would drive out demons. I still have two little hardback books given as prizes for first place in class. In IV Standard, *The Heroes*, with stories of Perseus slaying the Gorgon, Jason and the Argonauts, Theseus and the Minotaur. And in V Standard, *Pinocchio*, the classic tale by Carlo Collodi, where the foolish puppet ignores warnings not to listen to the advice of bad companions.

After this phase of dutiful schoolboy behaviour there came an inevitable ebbing away, the gradual onset of teenage academic decline and its associated distractions. In the coming years there would be new knacks to master, for instance, how to run across the street without suffering the ignominy of being seen to button your blazer. A complex manouevre performed by pressing thumb against the middle buttonhole, stretching out the middle finger, or forefinger, one finger only, to clutch the opposing button towards the thumbed opening, both sides of the jacket secured in a pincer movement, sufficient to prevent coat-tails flapping or coins hopping out of pocket. Older boys could carry this off with nonchalant ease. I can manage it still, as needs demand.

In that interim year, commuting from Cooley, my father drove my sister and me to school in the mornings, her to St Vincent's Convent, me to the Marist, and we made our own way home by bus. For me, this was the birth of the cool, hanging around under the redbrick wall of the cigarette factory opposite the Green Church, waiting for the Carlingford bus, singing with the big boys at the back of the bus. Anything could happen, but, alas, it didn't, or at least not to me.

The Marist was for day boys and boarders both, with minimal mutual contact. The boarders added a sense of mystique. What went on in the refectory, down those three steps where day boys never dared to venture? Where were their dormitories? Why were they divided into houses? Where were their parents? One new boarder boy, placed beside me in Prep A, sat with his blond head cradled in folded arms, inconsolable, and wept for a week. Nine years old, his parents were rumoured to be diplomats in the Far East. I don't remember whatever became of him after he calmed down, assuming he did calm down.

On Fridays, after school, my sister and I got a lift home with my father. Bovril with biscuits in his site office was a big part of our week, waiting for him to finish work, me drawing on the back of old blueprints under his desk or slipping out to wonder at the precision of the structure rising out of the ground. I didn't meet Ronnie Tallon then, architect of the GEC factory, winner of the RIAI Gold Medal, nor was I conscious of his control on site, but I could see there was something special being put together under my father's watchful eye. He set up his easel one day to make an abstract painting of the works on site. When, finally, I got to meet Tallon, on a visit to his finely detailed glass house, him painting watercolour squares in his old age, he told me of his appreciation for my father's concentrated attention to an important building of his early career.

I went on big days out with both my parents, with my mother to Dublin, with my father to roam in the mountains. Our days out in Dublin, after we'd been to the museum to see the dugout canoe, balanced almost out of sight on top of display cases, all forty-five feet of it, and after we'd marvelled at the leathery bogman, those days usually ended with a visit to the Wagon Wheel for chocolate eclairs before the train home. My mother had a taste for café life in the city, a taste I share. With my father I wandered up Maeve's Gap, climbed Slieve Foy and crossed Carlingford Lough to walk up as far as Cloch Mhór in the Mournes behind Rostrevor. We parked the car on the southern side, at a place called Narrow Water, and my father put thumb and forefinger in his mouth to produce a piercing whistle, another knack I didn't manage to inherit from that quiet man. Thus summoned, the boatman rowed across to ferry us over in the early morning mist, landing below the tower house on the other side. This handful of outings, whole days in the company of just one parent, was a privilege rarely granted and greatly appreciated, then and now.

I only recently discovered that my mother had not been thriving in the isolation of life in the country, not at all. Cooley was an earthly paradise for me, a place or state of emergence, with freedom and adventure all around, nothing to do but anything and everything I pleased. I was happy in the long summer days, independence found out in the fields. For her, it had the opposite effect, much too confining of her convivial nature, making her lonely for life in the town. She might have gone mad if they'd stayed any longer, driven to despair watching the farmer in his field across the road, bent over every day, always attired in his suit and hat, lifting stones out of the ground. How could I have been so blithely unperceptive? For children and the adults in their lives, life is lived at different levels of awareness. Too late I chastise myself for my lack of empathy, but then, ah Cooley, my elsewhere!

Benches at the Marist were similar to the old schoolhouse in Grange. Four to a row, books stored under flip-up flaps, inkpots like inverted top hats inset beside a recessed groove for dip pens and pencils. Each morning, one of us got to raise the wooden roller shutter on the teacher's cupboard at the back of the class and walk the ranks and files, refilling inkwells from the heavy bottle of Quink, the same routine as in the national school. One boy, at the end of the row, had the habit of stacking his books on the sloping surface of his desktop. If everybody shivered the seat as one, shaking the bench together, those books would slide down the slope to hit the floor with a bang and trouble would befall the unwitting innocent. He never seemed to learn. The same boy, at the end of the day, begged for any half-empty inkwells to be passed his way. His teeth would be stained blue on the way home.

Any minor misbehaviour clocked by the teacher, dropped books included, and you were out in the corridor. If spotted by the passing principal, known as the president, out came the strap, three on each hand. At the end of the week, the president patrolled the classrooms with an enormous ledger, the notebook, for the reading of notes. Notes were given for every subject, with an additional note for discipline at the teacher's discrimination. Read out in tones of reason and in alphabetical order, as if it were an objective law of nature, week by week. A note of 5 was excellent, 2 was deplorable – the full range seemed never to be extended to reach as low as 1. A note of 3 was punished with three slaps, three on each hand for a 2. This was automatic, impersonal, indifferently administered, and in practice it meant that unsatisfactory performance was rewarded with a routine beating. Infringement of discipline was, to some extent, inside everybody's own control, and punishment for 'dis' did not tend to become a pattern, being avoidable by luck or by stealth. It must have been transmitted in teacher training college that weakness at maths or poor spelling could be remedied by rough treatment from a leather strap. Since it was more or less the same line-up for beatings every week, the non-academic boys sought their retribution, perhaps reasonably so when considered in retrospect, as schoolyard bullies. The priests wore long black cassocks and most were able to draw their straps, from up their sleeves or out of their pockets, at surprising speed, whether from practised habit or native cunning. Some, it was rumoured, had their straps loaded with lead shot. The boy beside me was once taken upstairs to a priest's room for a special beating. He returned in a state of shock, his open palm having been strapped so furiously that he could not manage to make a fist and red-lumped bruises were beginning to protrude from the back of his hand. However, frightening as it was, such sadism did not so often arise in the junior school, these classes being single-teacher fiefdoms, where our all-round teacher knew all about each of us, and could moderate the system accordingly, so that fairness was a factor. But fear was never far off. It faded out in the upper years of the senior cycle, because the times were changing. But the middle years at the Marist were brutal, not for the brainy ones or the ones who knew how to stay out of trouble, but brutal for those few who fell victim and damaging too for the many who were forced to bear witness.

School life was not all bad, or not only bad. Marbles in the yard, gang life in the yard, fights at the back of the ball alleys, each day brought its moment of thrill. We went on an educational trip to the Hill of Tara, wholly invisible to us as a monument to past glories but wonderful for rolling down its grassy slopes. And to Slane, where, marvellously, the bell tower was open for climbing. We coaxed our tweed-suited and hefty teacher up the tiny winding stair until she got stuck at the hip, or found it difficult to move. And then, one after another, taking turns, each boy ran up the spiral stair until his head collided with her wide and tweedy behind 'Sorry, Miss Ward!' went the battle cry. The grassy site at Slane, where St Patrick lit the fire to antagonise the druids, was strewn with small boys collapsed into pagan laughter. Our antagonised teacher, a patient soul, took it in her stride.

One day, out of the blue, Sean Connery came to visit the brewery building works on site where my father was on duty. The visit was duly recorded in the local newspaper, a photo of Connery surrounded by an admiring group of girls, not quite Bond girls, but girls who looked happy to be there. After the visit, he needed a lift to some further reception at a nearby hotel and he rode in the back of my father's Vauxhall Viva. Hearing of this, just a few hours later, I went out to be on my own in the car, to absorb the allure. 'He's balder than you'd think,' I was told by my slowly balding father. 'Yes, quite a bit balder.' In the middle of the back seat, there it lay, discarded but intact – an empty packet of Player's Navy Cut, the sailor's choice for Commander Bond. I touted the relic in a procession around the schoolyard next day. Not that it was signed or in any way authenticated, but my father had vouched that Connery sat alone for those few minutes in the back of the car. One by one, in reverence, boys of all ages, friend and foe, asked to be allowed to hold the cigarette packet that had been held in the hand, must have fallen from the suit pocket, of 007. We all, each one of us, everybody, had the Corgi car of course, complete with ejector seat, bullet-proof shield, retractable guns, tyre-slashing blades – but this event was as close as it got to the man himself. That day I was the one who had nearly met, had come that close to meeting, Bond, James Bond, and who had the granting of the hold of his empty packet of twenty Player's – 'Player's Please'.

Despite the house moves, changes of school and social dislocation, one factor of continuity, one irreducible image, of those first ten years emerges to hold the whole thing together: summer holidays spent camping in tents or caravans in the west of Ireland, in Kerry and Mayo, but most often on the beaches of Connemara. These annual holidays were probably short in reality, and maybe not strictly annual, but in memory they stretch to infinity.

There were strenuous preparations and long car journeys to be endured, but none of the tedium of all this palaver sticks in the mind. It is the feeling of untrammelled freedom, all together as a unit with ample space to be alone, sand dunes to chase through, boulders to clamber over, rock pools to stare into, periwinkles to pick, campfire cooking, stories read by torchlight, the whispering and giggling that goes on undercover in a dark tent. Down on the campsite at the back of Dog's Bay, stepping away from the high doorstep of our butty little caravan, my father would tie a long string around a large potato, to send it sky-high, launched into orbit over the rolling dunes. My sister and I set off in pursuit of the so-called 'Spudnik', scouring the sandhills and hollows for the missing satellite, while, I suppose, my parents must have found a few moments' peace. Another year, he built a piano-shaped sand yacht, assembled from prefabricated plywood sections cut to shape upstairs in the box room in Cooley. With blue and orange sails flapping in the sea breeze, carried on three red wheelbarrow wheels, we went whizzing along the three-mile length of the long strand at Inch. Another summer, I tied long reins of twine through the jaws of a short blue shark found recently dead, possibly a porbeagle, bloated but not yet putrid, floating in the shallow waters of Dooagh Beach on Achill Island. I rode that shark like Danny on a Dolphin in the *Beano*, one hand holding fast to the dorsal fin, imagining I was out in the wild. That beach was later swept away in a storm, vanished completely for thirty-three years, until its sands returned in another storm. Clock time can never be reliable as a measure of discoveries made in real time, time flying by, slowing down, stretching out or standing stock still. Those childhood holidays in the west were days out of the ordinary calendar, immeasurable in their immensity, moments of solidarity stored away in the inner mind.

Far from Home

Sing to me of the man, Muse, the man of twists and
turns driven time and again off course ...

Homer, *The Odyssey*

WHEN I WAS NINE years old, I spent a short holiday at my
father's family home in the Spa, a few miles outside Tralee.
I wanted to ride the ponies with my cousins, all of them
expert in the saddle. I still have a letter, written in my
father's distinctive hand, sent from his site office, missing
me, reminding me, 'It's what you have wanted all along.'
The old house had been divided between my aunt's big
family and my solitary grandmother. Two semi-detached
households conjoined by the common ground of a long
conservatory, a lean-to glass porch original to the house,

overlooking a sunken lawn set out for tennis and croquet. The house was surrounded by tall trees with uncountable crows nesting in their branches. Nobody seemed to notice the constant cawing that sawed the air. I felt confused by my cousins' Kerry accents, a lonely stranger in my own land. I had wanted to find my homeplace. Now I wanted to go home.

My grandmother would emerge from her darkened lair to sit most of the day among the plants in the sunny porch. She had a parrot in a cage, brought back from his African adventures by my father's younger brother. I was interested in this exotic if unfriendly bird, pushing bits of toast and apple into his cage, poking my fingers through the bars. I was warned he would bite. When he sank his pointed beak into my finger, holding tight with his claw and waiting for the taste of a spot of blood before letting go, I must have been surprised, even a little upset. I took myself over to Nana's chair, seeking comfort or consolation. 'I told you he would bite,' she reminded me. No comfort offered. No consolation.

Years later, when I heard of the stand-off between my teenage father and his mother, her having lost her husband to the sea, her eldest son already gone off to sea, him now heading off to war against her wishes, her sworn promise of disinheritance if he joined the Navy, his name not earning even as much as a mention when her will was read, and all this despite their apparent closeness during my early childhood, I remembered my Nana's dispassionate words – 'I told you he would bite.'

I knew that my grandmother had long ago endured the grief of my grandfather's drowning off the coast of Brittany, leaving her with seven children to rear, perhaps hardening her heart, who knows. My grandfather must have been something of an adventurer, hobby sailing from Kerry to France, semi-smuggling shipments of brandy and butter to supply his spirit grocer shops in Tralee and Carlow. My father, who had sailed with him on some of these expeditions, was at that time beginning his final year as a boarder in Mungret College. He was summoned from study, told of the shipwreck, that his father hadn't been found, and summarily sent back to his desk. Three weeks later the body was washed up on the rocky shores of Plougrescant and quickly buried in the local churchyard, the grave since tended by local connections of the family business. No one there to tend to the turbulence of my father's teenage psyche. Blaming himself, he suffered what he later recognised as some sort of nervous breakdown, went, as he said, wild in his mind.

He first told me of this personal trauma as I drove him home from a family funeral, the funeral of his older brother, a man I hadn't met until his fading days. He was the living spit of my father, the same way of walking. He had joined the Merchant Navy on his father's firm advice just one year before the Brittany drowning and had not been seen and only rarely heard of in sixty years. This missing uncle had come home finally from his Merseyside exile to take over the family-owned hotel on the beach at Inch. Stationed here, trusted by a growing coterie of surfers, waiting for their call, he would stare out of the window, his seaman's eye measuring the ocean swell, on the ready to report signs of surf coming up. Not a natural-born hotelier, he ran that old place steadily into the ground. His wake was held on a stormy night. A line of mourners sat in the dark of the hotel bar, the corpse laid out on a table, penny coins on his eyes to pay the ferryman, two cigarettes in his breast pocket for company, the glow of phosphorescence rising from the rolling waves below. We helped carry his coffin out into the hearse, bracing each other against the gusts of wind and blasts of driving rain.

The next day, in the downpour of a rain-washed graveyard in Tralee, my father stood beside me, sharing the shelter of an undertaker's black umbrella. The black-coated funeral director, under another of his outsized umbrellas, having noisily closed and locked the iron door of the family vault, called out to the gathering in ominous tones, 'Who takes the key?' I might have expected my father to step forward, him being next in line alive at the time, but just then he seemed to have disappeared into thin air. After a short hesitation, my uncle's eldest son indicated agnate acceptance of that solemn responsibility. As the mourners dispersed, I turned to find my father quietly tucked in behind me, still under the umbrella, but safely out of sight. His vanishing act seemed to signal a silent determination never to join his coffined relatives on the shelves of their brick-built mausoleum.

Long car journeys, facing outwards in the same direction, shoulder to shoulder, not face to face, can be conducive to new conversations. He told me, as we drew near to our Dundalk destination, 'I'll be buried in the town where I work, where I belong.'

Seventeen years ago, I went to visit my grandfather's grave, in the little village of Plougrescant on the western tip of France, within sight and sound of waves smashing on the skerries. Those tide-hidden rocks must have been the site of the wreckage. I found a board-marked concrete headstone with packing-crate stencilled lettering; *David Tuomey, died at sea, August 1938.* I rang my father on my mobile, to say here I was, standing at the well-kept graveside with my son, his grandson, the age now that he was then, four generations of Tuomey men connected down the line. Had he set up the painted concrete headstone?

Silence. Then two sentences, with a pause in between.

'I have nothing to do with that grave.'

'My mother should have brought the body home.'

So maybe it's not unrelated that my father rushed off to join the British Navy the next year, ditching the first year of his university studies, and maybe he had reason to accept his mother's resolute response. He had six weeks to wait, working on building sites in Belfast, sharing a bed with a man who worked night shifts, waiting for his eighteenth birthday to allow him to join up. He first trained in radar, then aircraft navigational training, finally, towards the end of the war, flying into narrow fjords to lay aerial mines, preventing Norwegian waters being used to harbour German U-boats. In August 1944 his ship, the Canadian-crewed aircraft carrier HMS *Nabob*, was torpedoed below the waterline by one of those enemy submarines. According to the Royal Navy Research Archive, thirty men died and a further forty were injured in that attack. Six years to the month after his father's drowning in the cruel sea, my father found himself floating in the Arctic waters of the Barents Sea, one of 205 survivors taken aboard the escort *Algonquin*. Not that he ever mentioned the war; like so many of his generation, the whole empty adventure was not up for easy reminiscence.

Once, after teaching at the Røros summer school, having toured those same fjords with our host Hans Skotte, him recounting boyhood discoveries of washed-up mines, having been told by his parents how those mines had kept them safe, I returned to my father with spirit-restoring reports of Norwegian gratitude for the Allied actions. It was then he handed over the photograph album that has allowed me to piece together his time in the war. Scanning a formal photo of the 852 Squadron, I found him standing in the fourth row, arms folded, cap tilted, ready for action. In February 1944, he had gone to join his ship in San Francisco, shipped over to America on the *Queen Mary* freshly stripped out for the troops, returning to a Clyde shipyard via the Panama Canal.

I don't remember feeling like crying when my father died, his eventual death being a welcome end to his slow removal from conscious life by confusion of mind. One afternoon in London, six years after his funeral, I came upon a short aerial film in the *Ocean Liners* exhibition at the Victoria and Albert Museum, a newsreel showing thousands of sailors out on the deck of the *Queen Mary*. I knew he must be there somewhere, one among those tiny specks of humanity heaving from side to side like mechanically animated figures. And there, anonymous among the many in attendance, I wept without warning for my long-lost old man.

You Don't Know Me

You think you know me well
But you don't know me
Eddy Arnold and Cindy Walker, 'You Don't Know Me'

'YOU DON'T KNOW ME, you don't speak to me, you don't come near me at all!' So hissed my sister, in a low whisper, as we walked in the door of the disco. After a lot of pleading from me, my mother had given way. I was allowed out to my first dance, a hop at the badminton club, grudgingly considered safe for me to go, with the protective company of my older sister. My sister, having said nothing to the contrary at the time, turned out to have different plans. I was left to slink around the dark sides of the dance floor all evening, reuniting with her only when it was time to go home. Message understood, no fight with my sister. We survived the night, each in our own way. I'd got to see the lights and hear the music. I was on the road to freedom.

I had begun to be distracted by the power of popular music while we still lived in Cooley, so I must have been about nine years old when I fell in love with Elvis. Pictures and posters cut out of music magazines covered the walls of my bedroom, with one special double-page fold-out, with his blue-black hair and red shirt, his turned-up collar and his curled-up lip, stuck centrally over the mantelpiece. I see it still if I close my eyes, the gloss of perfection cruelly disfigured by one blacked-in gap in the pearly white teeth, my father's idea of a joke, not a funny one, not at all. I was a registered member of the Elvis Presley Fan Club, a regular subscriber to *Elvis Monthly* magazine, the shy-proud wearer of a badge, the gold disc surmounted by the royal crown, small enough to pin under the lapel of my school blazer, hidden out of sight, the King being regarded as yesterday's man by the boys in the yard, but I had the secret power of knowing it was there. Sorahan's record shop in Park Street signed me up for a steady supply of singles, starting with 'That's All Right' / 'Blue Moon of Kentucky', his first record, released the year I was born. I loved the special sound of Scotty Moore's guitar, and the Jordanaires, and also the sound of their name. The one and only sound of Elvis's voice, also his speaking voice. I can still see the list of songs handwritten in the order book lying open on the shop counter, 'It's Now or Never', 'Are You Lonesome Tonight?', 'She's Not You', Mr Sorahan's own selection brought in one at a time to suit my pocket money, 'Viva Las Vegas' being last on the list before Elvis was supplanted in my affections and the big shift to the Beatles began with 'I Want to Hold Your Hand'.

It was a sign of schoolyard one-upmanship to be able to list off song names from forthcoming LPs before anyone had heard the actual record. This was one advantage of fan club membership, with the added holy-picture value of autographed photos of the band. The Who, The Stones, The

Move, each to his own. Crucial information was gathered from late-night radio with the under-the-pillow transistor tuned to Radio Luxembourg. Sorahan's sold the weekly *New Musical Express*, the *NME*, the sure source of inside knowledge. The two-word sound of 'Sexy Sadie', such a daringly provocative title, added mystique to the build-up to the release of the Beatles' *White Album*, the song itself not mattering so much when the real thing came along.

What a pity that so many of the lovely poems learned by heart in English and Irish classes have long left my mind, while the lyrics of songs never studied, songs that seemed to promise that love was just around the corner, lodge in memory's crevices, lying in wait like conger eels, ready to come alive out of the deep dark, word-for-word, whenever some old tune comes on the car radio. One day, not too long ago, I had to stop the car, overcome by the emotional reverberations of 'Private Number', a flood of feeling rushing back after all these years. The Friday night crescendo of high-stepping camaraderie at the Friary Club used to culminate in dancing together to 'Let's Work Together', that catchiest of catchy songs by Canned Heat. Why do these simple songs stick in the mind?

Our French teacher took the pre-Inter Cert class on a mid-term trip to Paris. The lycée prepared different and delicious regional dishes every night, boeuf bourguignon, Provençal chicken and so on. One of the boarders, a maths wizard as I recall, refused to eat any of this foreign food and survived the week on a plain diet of French bread and Coca-Cola. Another boy, a non-swimmer, wanting to keep up with the show-offs in the swimming pool, launched himself head first into the shallow end of the pool and split his forehead open from side to side. He was stitched up and back in action by the end of the day. Not much opportunity to practise our French conversation on that study trip, but luckily there was a girls' school tour from Dublin staying across the courtyard and I was befriended by a slightly older girl. We sat together on a bench, well hidden behind the waterfall in the Bois de Vincennes, and practised our French kissing late into the night. I limped home to the lycée those evenings, stricken with the puzzling pain of newly tender balls.

Dundalk was a factory town, its redbrick terraces remaining from the reputedly great days of the Great Northern Railway. The repetitive street lines and the precision of those engineering bricks gave the town a hard-edged feeling. We lived in a big redbrick house not far from the railway station. I spent a fair amount of time hanging around in the station, running up and down the long wooden-floored ramp, playing bar billiards in the waiting room off the glass-canopied platform, climbing over the huge steam engine stored away in the dark of its shed, forgotten in the sidings. That railway station, from where I journeyed back and forth during my student days, dark nights on an empty train arriving on the bright platform, still makes me feel at home, more at home than most other places in the town. I like those red bricks of the railway terraces still, more orange than red in reality, it's true. And admittedly, yes, the station itself is built in yellow brick, with only linear stripes of red, but that can be forgiven as an exception to the rule. Nothing soft about them, these red bricks, angular in outline, northern in character. We have built with them in Dublin and Belfast, London and Liverpool.

I measured the main street, Clanbrassil Street, for a geography practical project, drawing adjoining elevations in sharpened pencil, approximately accurate, house by house, both sides of the street facing each other across one long roll of white cartridge paper. There were families living upstairs over most of the shops in that street: pharmacists, drapers, bankers, multi-generational households comfortably accommodated, usefully observing, with what we now call passive surveillance, all the goings-on of the street life below. Many of my school friends lived over their parent's shops. Neither flats nor houses, they were working townhouses, once the norm in every street in town. These lived-in street buildings existed in a condition of interdependent exchange with the life of the town, night and day.

This schoolboy survey took me to a closer inspection of the courthouse, one of the best buildings in the town. I knew something of its layout from accompanying my father on his occasional court appearances as an expert witness, his office being just across the street from the courthouse. The public space of the town square extended uninterrupted into the open portico and continued from there to the stair hall, an axial sequence leading through covered spaces, covered but not enclosed, along stone floors, under painted ceilings and their cornices, interior stucco work sheltered from the wind and rain, surviving more than one hundred and fifty years in the otherwise open air. The first closed door that anyone had to open would have delivered citizens directly into the courtroom itself, or, up at the top of an open stair, to the visitors' gallery. The space in between, the path from street to room, was an extended threshold connecting the day-to-day life of the building with the world outside. A democratic architecture, solidly civic, true in its ethos to its Greek-inspired origins.

Dundalk weekdays started to the sequenced sounds of hooters and sirens, different tones from low whines rising to short whistle blasts, calling hundreds of workers to the breweries, tobacco works or shoe factories. A tough enough town then, but there was something softer, even poetical about the environs, plenty to keep a preoccupied boy occupied. Behind our redbrick house was a copse of tall trees known as 'the clump', long since cleared of its trees and blandly grassed over, then a circular wood big enough to get lost in, with sycamore trees easy enough to climb. Sitting up among the swaying branches in the treetops, you could see back to Cooley. High up here was the place to plan raids on the nearby hills, three mythical places visible from this vantage point: Cúchulainn's Castle, where the hero was supposed to have been born and is said to have buried all his riches; Tippings Wood, a wooded knoll on the way out to Cooley; and Úrchnoc Chéin mhic Cáinte, site of an ancient bardic school on the road towards Castle Roche.

I recently heard the poet Nuala Ní Dhomhnaill talking on the radio about a car journey with her daughter to see Eamhain Macha, the seat of the kings of Ulster, just north of Dundalk. Her daughter had asked whether all these legendary kings and heroes had ever really existed. The poet replied that nobody could say for sure whether there had really been such men, but we all knew for certain where each one of them was born and the exact location of the stones that marked where they were buried. In the case of Cúchulainn, any lingering uncertainty concerning the burial place of the warrior hero is surely resolved by the satisfactory presence of a handsomely rounded and upright granite monolith, standing solitary in a sloping field to the right of the tree-shaded lane leading up to the mount, the mount that bears his name.

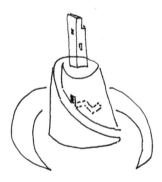

Aged about eleven, covertly engaged in a summer's expeditionary campaign with a friend from school, we crawled deep into the narrow souterrain under Cúchulainn's Castle, further in each day as courage allowed, down the stone-lined slope and around two angled bends as far as the blocked end of the thirty-metre shaft, the compacted clay of that closing wall impervious to our scrapings, no treasure to be found. By the light of our torches, using my father's surveying tapes and folding rules, we made a map. Maybe it's still hidden where we left it, under the floorboards of my bedroom in the family home. When I see the tiny mouth of that passageway, halfway up the curved ramp that wraps around the earthen mound, its iron gate blocked up now, barred against any more boys, it makes me shiver to think how much time we spent sliding along on our bellies, head first, down inside that dark tunnel.

The mount is surrounded by a ditch, deep and wide, with huge trees overhanging it. One big sycamore, quite near the entry to the souterrain, had a knotted rope looped over an upper branch, its loose end dangling just within reach. From here, emerging from the narrow darkness, it was a short run and jump to swing out wide across the chasm, sailing through the dappled light of the tree canopy, aiming to land softly on the other side. A safe landing depended on remembering to let go of the rope just in time, otherwise you had to let yourself drop three-quarters way across the pendulum's swaying arc and slither down the sloping bank or, worse, suffer the humiliation of being hauled back to the wall from where you came. Best to trust in the moment of letting go and avoid the risk of a climb down. Another shiver whenever I see the time-worn rope marks scarred in the bark of that tree.

With the same friend, armed with the same torches, I went to a Saturday matinee screening of one of Boris Karloff's Frankenstein movies at the almost empty Magnet Cinema. The torches were for reading comics in the dark, a precaution against moments when the movie might get too scary. They had green and red plastic adjustable lens covers to dim the illumination, with a blue-tinted cylinder sliding over the bulb to focus the torchlight down to a pencil-narrow beam. These were cheap but perfect accessories, an adornment to any adventurer's trouser belt. But those torches provided no defence against the horror of the creature's stumbling advance, his heavy-booted stomping with arms outstretched, heading straight at us down the cinema's central aisle. We jumped out of our seats and ran for our lives, ran the half-mile home without a backward look. Brave enough we were to carry those multi-coloured torches down the winding tunnel on our myth-driven quest for treasure, but we were terrified by the life-threatening reality presented by the black-and-white picture show.

The following year, on the few days I didn't feel ready to cycle out with everybody else to the Blackrock swimming pool, rare days of abstinence from the concrete seawater pool that was the social hub of every summer holiday, I would cycle instead to Tippings Wood, climb over the stone boundary wall and scramble through the forest undergrowth to reach the bare bald summit, where the herons nested, and spend an idle afternoon alone on that lofty lookout, hours wasted, far from wasted, keeping watch over the ancient outline of the Cooley Mountains. The cultural landscape of the Táin Bó Cúailnge, legendary site of the Cattle Raid of Cooley, long-ago battleground that cost Cúchulainn his hero's life. Like any hero, Greek or Gael, if he ever was, he always is

Then, a little further on, when I was about fourteen, I walked out of town with my girlfriend to read aloud the poem we'd been working on at school, a poem written about this very place, 'Úrchnoc Chéin Mhic Cáinte' by Peadar Ó Doirnín, an eighteenth-century figure more famous for his lyrics set to music in Seán Ó Riada's 'Mná na hÉireann'. Our Irish teacher, a priest with a passion for poetry, brought into class bundles of reel-to-reel tapes he'd collected from native speakers' recitations. He had inspired me to read outside the curriculum, lending me an old and tattered copy of *Tóraíocht Dhiarmada agus Ghráinne*. As if he believed that the English novel would be wasted on boys, our wooden-legged English teacher passed over most of the set prose but kept the pressure on the poetry, with long passages hammered into us by daily repetition. Immersion in Gaelic eroticism, prolonged exposure to Wordsworth's pantheism, combined with all this locally charged mythology of castles and mounds, passageways and forests, led to that rainy day's poetry reading under the trees, where I had hoped my own pursuit, *mo thóraíocht féin*, might lead to closer contact with my newfound girlfriend. If the poem's promise of a return to nature was to be believed, we should have lain down naked like lovers in the leaves, but such taboo-breaking touching would have been beyond us both, so we held hands ardently in the rain-wetted wood.

I recite to myself now, as the dark days of this second winter lead towards our release from Covid confinement, as we approach the first day of spring, the opening lines of Antoine Ó Raifteirí's poem 'Cill Aodáin' that we all learned at school:

> *Anois teacht an earraigh*
> *Beidh an lá dul chun síneadh*
> *Is tar éis na féil' Bríde*
> *Ardóidh mé mo sheol.*

Brigid's Shrine at Faughart, birthplace of Saint Brigid, is a low-lying place full of mystery. If she was born anywhere, she was born here. You can visit the holy well where the saint plucked out her eye to spoil her beauty, to keep her suitors at bay. You can put your finger in the hole in the stone, the smoothly rounded socket where she placed the discarded eyeball. And you can place your knees in the two circular hollows where the stone was worn away from her constant kneeling and praying. This is not the site where she spread her cloak to cover all the ground needed to found a convent. That is in Kildare. But nearby, at Long Woman's Grave, is a similar myth-laden, land-stretching situation. A local chieftain showed his Spanish lady all the land he owned, as far as the eye could see, and the sight of that mountainy bog caused her to pass away in shock. 'Here she sleeps today, in the hollow of her disappointment' according to the local tourist office website. The Louth landscape is soaked in legend.

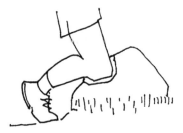

Retreats were a regular element in the school calendar, run by visiting Redemptorist priests, roaring from the pulpit, hectoring their captive audience with the fear and dangers of divine retribution, but it didn't cut deep. We were already quite accustomed to hours of silent study. The annual retreat merely extended the rule of silence across a whole day. Compensation for this extra time in no-conferring confinement could be found in the cardboard box of pamphlets, suitable religious reading material spread out on trestle tables at the end of the study hall. Scattered among these staple-bound papers, mostly dull documents intended to lead young minds away from dwelling on erotic thoughts, were the impossibly exotic stories of the lives of the saints. Printed on thin paper, written in urgent prose, with gushing descriptions full of passion and ecstasy, these stories left a lasting impression. Francis of Assisi, who gave everything away. Anthony of Padua, who could be relied on to find and return whatever was lost. Catherine of Siena, whose mummified head is preserved in her home town, twenty-fourth of twenty-five children, an illiterate mystic who prayed, pleaded and eventually succeeded in her campaign for the pope's return to Rome, where her headless body lies under the altar of the Basilica of Santa Maria sopra Minerva. Borromini's church of Sant'Agnese in Agone is filled with shrines and side altars devoted to the memory of the martyrs. Saint Cecilia, for example, who having survived unsuccessful attempts to steam her to death, was said to have been killed by a single slice from an axe. Centuries later, her body was uncovered, uncorrupted, in its Roman crypt in the catacombs, then buried again in a church of her own name in Trastevere. To add to the complexity of this saint's story, there seems to be scant evidence supporting her patronage of musical performers.

Nowadays, for me, no trip to Italy can be considered complete without a visit to the shrine of one or other of those miraculous heroes of the silent retreat. Catherine of Siena, having lived in a time of plague, died on 29 April 1380. Strange to call it a feast day for a saint who had stopped eating and drinking, her appetite for physical life lost, her mystical vision undimmed. That her remains lie preserved in Rome is only partly true. Different body parts – head, thumb, three fingers, a foot, shoulder blade and rib – have found their way into various churches in Florence, Venice and, of course, her homeplace of Siena. Whatever remains of her remains is splendidly interred in her sepulchre in the sopra Minerva.

And so it was, in Rome, six and a half centuries later, on 29 April 2022, as the current of the current pandemic seemed about to ebb, I found myself joining the line of pilgrims in the sopra Minerva, working our way around the back of the altar, crouching one by one through the low door beneath the table. When my turn came to shuffle under, I knelt with my hand on the recumbent statue's cold stone shoulder, but held back from kissing the cheek of the effigy as others had done. Strange in its way to kiss the cheek, given the headless reality of the body buried beneath. The story of Catherine's childhood visions had held a certain appeal for my teenage self. Had I not had my own visions in the back garden in Drumshanbo? Had I not stood waiting in the fields of Cooley for the sky to open behind sun-setting god-beams? And, since we'd learned something about ecstasy in English class, in the real world outside retreats, what difference in substance stood between Catherine's relentless mania and Wordsworth's wonder at a mountain looming down over a lake? Not that I was driven by these dimly registered visions to see the thing through with fasting and prayer, but inside myself I could relate to the sensitivities of such a soul. Kneeling there, under the table, I felt again a fleeting connection with the sacred, a chance to credit early glimpses of inspiration, grateful for the comforting component of transcendence, paying my respects, when in Rome.

A less comfortable moment in my coming to sense came when my mother had all her children lined up beside her in the Marist Church in Dundalk, ready for the Good Friday ritual of kissing the five wounds, the speared side, nailed feet and hands of the crucifix, the silver cross held out by one of the cruellest priests in school. That Easter marked a mini-crisis in my disengagement with the divine, or with the clerical control of the divine. Row by row the congregation filed up to the altar rails. My turn was coming fast, heart pounding, palms sweating. I couldn't do it, not then, not now, not bend the knee. No chance you could stay behind on the bench to sit it out unnoticed, because each row in turn emptied itself out into the aisle. In my inner mind I'd become an unbeliever, but hadn't yet come out fully at home. Having left the Church in spirit, I wasn't quite ready to stand up and leave the actual church, adding to my other troubles with my mother. So I did the practical thing and managed to faint, or feigned a fit of fainting. A friendly priest in the aisle spotted me in my distress and helped me out by a side door, explaining to my mother how stuffy the church can get when crowded, and confiding to me, *sotto voce*, that we can all have our doubts.

Priests and lay teachers were known by their nicknames: Moses, Gonk, Fishy, Bulldog. Nicknames surely not self-applied, though I suppose all our teachers must have been aware of their own nicknames, derived from distortions of their given names, summations of inherent flaws or momentary failings, some perceived weakness in personality, or from origins obscure and long forgotten. Those most feared and those most loved were known, mostly, by their real names. One gentle and erudite teacher, no nickname as I recall, was routinely tormented, pelted with orange peel and wet paper missiles at the start of class, while his back was turned to set out that day's history lesson on the blackboard.

Wearily he would continue with his low-volume lecture, oblivious, resigned, unperturbed, slowly wearing down his besiegers, patiently ignoring their barbarian invasions into the civilised territory of his classroom.

Bullies were a condition of the school environment, a not insignificant danger, although much less so for a day boy, their reign having no reach outside the school walls. Punishments were random in the main, with no predictable pattern. Unprovoked, you might find yourself picked on in a passing attack, getting dead-legged in the line-up for class after break, causing you to fall out of line and then, in turn, finding yourself picked on by the priest or prefect in charge. Or, painfully, hauled off down the sports field, held steady by many hands, with the sun's rays slowly focused through a magnifying glass onto your bare leg, struggling to stifle any squeals until the smell of singed skin signalled the torture's end. Or, humiliatingly, hung up in the cloakroom by the hood and shoulders of your duffel coat, hanging from high hooks, handily exposed for a well-aimed dig in the ribs. Or, ridiculously, held down on the tarmac while the kingpin bully's weasel-faced sidekick, Willie-the-wind, a boy who could fart at will, squatted on your chest and let off a stinker in your upturned face. In junior school years I had managed to find a safe spot as captain of one out of any number of schoolyard gangs, a local leader among a cohort of my own kind, factions formed out of friendly rivalry. In those days a pocketful of marbles went a long way. Survival was not so simple in the savage jungle of the secondary cycle.

One long-suppressed moment of shameful difficulty was provoked out of hiding by the sight of Charles Ray's *Boy with Frog*, a public sculpture positioned most provocatively at the prow of the Dogana at the Venice Biennale 2009, then seen again more recently at Ray's retrospective at the Metropolitan Museum in New York. The boy stands naked, his belly pushed out, a frog held aloft and dangling by one leg from the clenched fist of his outstretched arm. This larger-than-life boy looks strangely innocent, evil maybe, or merely aloof. Whatever is ambiguous about the attitude of the boy, the frog looks to be in frightful danger.

Between the handball alleys, always the nerve centre of the Marist yard, and a rarely used Gothic Revival chapel-like building, there stood a small copse of trees. And one day, gathered in a circle under cover of those trees, a group of boys were tossing a sizeable frog back and forth, playing a cruel game of catch with the helpless creature.

At some point, and this must be why the sculpture jogged my memory, one boy, swinging his arm high in the air for a longer lob across the circle, found himself left holding on to the severed leg of the frog, detached from its torso by the rotational force of the throw. Watching from the sidelines, I was uneasy, fear rising to anger.

Out in the fields of Cooley I had developed a friendly relationship, even a self-adjudged fellowship, with frogs. I knew to cool my hands with water before handling these amphibians, so as not to burn their bellies. It was fun to scoop them up, hold them face to face, to stare through my thick glasses at their bulging eyes, my specky-four-eyes admiring their speckled backs, impressive to watch them hop off through wet grass and swim fast in a shallow stream. So now suddenly, without thinking, I stepped into the ring, the injured animal wriggling mutilated on the muddy ground, and smashed it dead with a stone. Everybody was horrified by this vicious intrusion into what, in their eyes, was only an idle game. For the rest of the week, I was unpopular as a pariah, reviled for my ruthless response, a stupid spoilsport, mocked for being squeamish and derided as a self-appointed and vengeful executioner – 'Who killed the frog?', 'Tuomey killed the frog!', 'Squashed it flat with a stone!' I was isolated. Out of step with the schoolyard. I had transgressed the common law. Charles Ray's problematic sculpture brought back the bitter taste of bile and confusion, feeling misunderstood, sorry for myself, the whole unpleasant incident resurfacing from the murky pond of memory. The sin of pride, again.

And then, back in the Cooley days, those early days, there was the story of my sister and the frog. A much less shameful story. Shameless. My middle sister, four years my junior, so she would have been four, was playing with a newly arrived pet rabbit in the vegetable garden, my father nearby and digging. I came across a little frog in the grass and dropped it down the neck of her jumper. She screamed in shock, wailed in disgust. My father, protective, furious, snatched up the nearest stick and smacked me smartly on the hand. Told me to get away out of the garden and stay well out of the house for the rest of the day. Took my sister into the kitchen for comfort. Banished to the bottom of the Green Field, I saw that I was bleeding from the palm of my hand, quite a bit of blood, quite a satisfying sight. Must have been a splinter in the stick. It was my father's fault. Perfect. I came dancing up to the kitchen door, smearing my bloody hand against the glass, running off again saying, 'No! I can't come in to put a plaster on it. How can I? I'm not allowed in the house all day.' Make them pay.

Dancing about Architecture

Writing about music is like dancing about architecture –
it's a really stupid thing to want to do.
                                        Elvis Costello, 1983

Dancing about Architecture is a Reasonable Thing to Do
                                        Joel Heng Hartse, 2022

THERE WASN'T MUCH MUSIC in our house when I was
growing up. A few favourite records and family holiday
sing-songs and, of course, the radio on night and day, but
not much live performance, apart from my father singing
Fenian songs, plaintive rebel songs, picking up a harmonica
to play 'The Coolin' or another slow air. I got a guitar in my
fourth year at secondary school, learned a few chords, no
talent for playing or singing, just enough nerve to perform
a simple song at a party. One Saturday night I ventured
into the Conradh na Gaeilge youth club, high up in a tall
terraced house in Seatown Place, to find myself fallen in
with a slightly older crowd, a year or two ahead of me in
school. No Irish language spoken that I could hear, but
these regulars seemed to have the run of the place. Boys
finger-picking steel string guitars, Mississippi blues on the
record player, nothing Irish or traditional, red lightbulbs
glowing in the floor lamps. At the piano, playing boogie-
woogie, was a girl I didn't know, but I gradually got her to

notice me by sitting down on the floor next to the piano for most of the night. I walked her home, strolling along on either side of my bicycle. Soon after that we started going out. Saturday night dates at the Adelphi Cinema and afterwards on to the Afton Club. Sunday night jam sessions in her family living room, me strumming three-chord ballads from the foot of the stair, she vamping along on the piano, her sisters taking turns to sing and play, her father smoothly intervening with jazz standards on saxophone and clarinet, his old jazz-band instruments retrieved out of battered cases, assembled from interlocking parts, insecurely held together with elastic bands. He was fluent too on the fiddle and tin whistle. There was a warm and enveloping intimacy, a greater intergenerational informality than I was used to, all kinds of music happily shared in that musical house. I began to understand that music, even lowdown everyday music, might be a higher form of human communication. 'Just direct your feet to the sunny side of the street.'

After the Inter Cert exams I was brought to the double-fronted draper's shop on Clanbrassil Street to be fitted for a new suit. A sign of manhood. My father said I needed to get used to wearing the armour I'd be wearing for the rest of my life, a gloomy prediction that happily didn't come true. The suit was double-breasted by my own design. In an inner room lined with shelves of grey material, I was measured up with a tailor's tape. Chest and shoulders, arms and inside leg. Then came a quietly asked and confidential question: 'Which side do you dress?' Took me a while to realise the meaning, unaware as yet of any bias, but I answered as the situation demanded, man to man. I'd called in many times to that multi-chambered shop, waiting in the wings while my girlfriend flicked through racks of dressmaking patterns. She made herself a pair of satin hot pants, short and tight. Too short and tight for her father to tolerate, she was sent back upstairs to change into something decent before we'd be allowed out for the night. She appeared again soon, smiling cheerfully and swinging about in a full-length skirt. Walking downtown towards the Afton, she ducked into a doorway to re-emerge in the hot pants she'd kept hidden under her skirt. Those hot pants were made to shine on the dance floor.

I took my first unsupervised trip to Dublin, nominated as a school delegate to the annual Vincent de Paul conference held in All Hallows College. After an hour or so I slipped away, skipping the Saturday evening session to go for fish and chips in Drumcondra, then headed round the corner to a disco at 'the Blind' – St Joseph's School for the Blind, another walled institution, just over the wall from All Hallows. Walked a girl home all the way along the dark and tree-lined Griffith Avenue. Got in late and slept in late, missing Sunday mass and most of the morning sessions of the conference. In Talbot Street, on the way to catch the Monday morning train, I stopped to buy a black corduroy Donovan cap, a look he'd borrowed from Bob Dylan, but as yet unobtainable in the shops of Dundalk. My first solo outing to Dublin, signifying the beginnings of an escape from school routine. Going home, as the train crossed the Drogheda viaduct, I was surprised to notice quite a few people, without comment, otherwise disconnected from each other, rise from their seats to open the sliding window and drop a coin into the Boyne, a good luck gesture immortalised around this time in Van Morrison's 'Madame George', that northern song not yet known to me.

Not that we often ventured north of the border. Despite Dundalk's midway location, the distance to Belfast seemed twice as far as Dublin. A couple of walking trips along the northern shores of Carlingford Lough with my father. One school trip to the ludicrously over-scaled Stormont, around the time Jack Lynch drove north to meet Captain Terence O'Neill and we heard how his car got snowballed by some of Paisley's supporters. Otherwise, it was another country. Many of the boarders in the Marist came from over the border, further increasing our distance from them and theirs from us. They were likely sent south to keep them out of trouble, out of harm's way. There was one special summer's day cycling expedition to Newry, returning with pocketfuls of Ugly Stickers chewing gum and just a few condoms. The ugly stickers, it told you on the pack, were 'for books, walls and bikes'. The condoms had an even higher street value in school. They could be filled from the swan neck taps in the upstairs science labs, then dropped out the high windows to fall down as water bombs into the yard. Hilarious fun. Further snickers of hilarity when some poor priest, having found the burst remains, took it as a worrying sign of inappropriate after-school activities happening in school grounds, and, very awkwardly, raised the matter as a moral concern at morning assembly.

Later in my working life, engagement in practice and teaching led to frequent cross-border contact. Across my professional career I've worked on a number of public projects in Northern Ireland, for client bodies from different political constituencies: liberal Belfast, nationalist Derry, unionist Coleraine, affluent Clandeboye. In each case, the sense of welcome to 'the province' was explicit; moreover, there was an implicit appeal that any new building should be open, democratic, acting as a future-facing agent of change, a more urgent expectation than the functional briefs encountered elsewhere. The North has become a big part of my life, with many good friends in the arts and architectural education. But back in my schooldays, living that close to the border, we weren't encouraged to cross the line.

One more Dublin visit was to an eye doctor in Fitzwilliam Square, where I was told I'd failed a standard test for stereoscopic vision, which failing, the specialist reassured me, shouldn't have any negative impact on my prospects, as long as I didn't intend to study architecture. He had a wooden figure of a monkey, an articulated contraption dangling by one arm from the mantelpiece. I distracted myself with the monkey while my father paid the bill. Neither of us mentioned my secret ambition. In practice, it's proved to be an easy disability to defeat, the disadvantage of one eye outperforming the other. You can read three dimensions in space by simply moving your head.

Although I was sprightly enough, could run over rocks, jump ponies over fences, climb trees with agility and was an active participant in annual sports day events, I never thrived at any team games at school, no eye for a ball, no good at football, not even in goal. The few efforts I made to join in on the pitch, cajoled into togging out for Wednesday afternoon Gaelic football matches, left me lonely and miserable, talking to myself and trailing along the muddy sidelines. Another attempt to join in, this time at basketball practice, went badly. The coach threw the ball straight at my face, knocking my glasses to the ground, shouting 'You'll have to learn to do without those if you want to play basketball!' I missed out on the benefit of any of the lessons that are said to be learned from team sports. We had weekly physical training sessions in the school hall, arm-stretching, knee-bending, toe-touching, press-ups and sit-ups. This enjoyable drill was delivered by a military man, an army sergeant brought over from the barracks, impersonal, barking out orders with his back to the wall. White-vested boys lined up in rows, arm's length apart, individuals co-ordinated on command, willing participants in a collective choreography. I've resurrected the discipline of this workout in recent days, beginning most mornings with arms outstretched, clenching and unclenching fists, then arms windmilling, carrying these bend and stretch actions through to the finale of press-ups and planks. This waking warm-up represents one element of silent continuity with schooldays gone by, following soldiers' orders still heard in my head, muscle memories of the mind.

I spent a good deal of my senior school winters stuck indoors with seasonal bronchitis, having to keep up with studies at home, housebound for weeks at a time, isolated from the school routine, kept apart from social life on a Saturday night, staying in every day except for Sunday family excursions out in the fresh air. Affected by these confining times, I might have seen myself living a somewhat introverted teenage life – what teenager doesn't? – listening to records at home, writing rhyming love lines, learning a few more chords on the guitar. I was an extrovert introvert. Optimistic by nature. Then again, melancholic betimes. But there's comfort in melancholy, as Joni Mitchell later explained. Friends would call to the house after school and we'd lie on the floor in an upstairs den, staring at the ceiling, dreamily undepressed by Leonard Cohen's *Songs from a Room*, singing along with the soundtrack to *Easy Rider*, mesmerised by the strange sounds of *In the Court of the Crimson King*, haunted by the Moody Blues' *Days of Future Passed*, minds fixed on the freedoms of days to come.

My mother might have harboured hopes for me to be an engineer like my father, to join my father's practice, father and son working together in a family firm, the energy of youth and the experience of age, a dynamic combination. I had opposite plans. Specifically, especially, not to turn into my inward-turning father, silent fisherman, lone gardener, crossword puzzler, reader of Dante, Homer and the diaries of Samuel Pepys. Generally, I wanted to be of my own making and much more out in the world. The visible step ahead, the pathway out, moving on with what I'd learned from my father's discipline of measured drawings and land surveying, led towards architecture or, failing that, as a possible second preference, archaeology.

I joined the Old Dundalk Society. I began to understand buildings as evidence of human intelligence. Insights could be gained from standing within the ruins of medieval tower houses, observing pockets in the stonework where the floors had fallen out. My parents being members of the Louth Archaeological Society, we went together on their occasional field trips. One time, beautifully, climbing in single file down an iron ladder, through something like a well shaft, to walk in candlelit procession into the corbelled chamber of the as-yet unexcavated passage tomb at Dowth. Or, under the trained eye of a local teacher, finding Bronze Age rath systems revealed, uneventful green landscapes translated, in the sweep of an arm, into stories of what lay beneath. I've come to read the footprints of archaeological settlements as if they were building sites suspended in time. Rather than ruins sinking into the ground, I see structures rising into the air. And the strange thing is, I feel more at home with the potentiality of the stripped-down and fragmentary remains of Greek temples, more comfortable than I could ever be with the reputedly gilded splendour of their original finished state. Not simply a preference for a spartan reduction to essentials, but an ingrained inclination towards the space of the imagination.

I remember my father explaining the difference in activity between the two building professions, engineering and architecture. Engineers calculate structure, architects shape space. I had no sense yet of space as a thing in itself, apart from the infinity of outer space, or the more finite problem of not enough space in a schoolbag. No understanding of the space between freestanding objects, no concept of solid space as sculptural form. I knew something about building sites. And I had one big compendium book on the history of architecture, *World Architecture*, which gave me first sight of the Sydney Opera House, not to be experienced in reality for another fifty years. Seeing one photograph of Sydney made a singular impression, awe-inspiring to my innocent eye. I would spread that book out on the floor, maybe on a wet Sunday afternoon, and imagine being there, far away in Australia, standing under those arching concrete shells. Later, when I started teaching at UCD, listening to students with overly flamboyant hopes for perfectly everyday projects, I might sometimes softly suggest, to temper any tendency towards self-delusion – 'Well, let's see if we can agree, whatever it is, it's no Sydney Opera House!' So when I finally arrived in Sydney, it was with an uneasy suspicion – what if, after all these years, discovered in the flesh, the thing itself turned out to be no Sydney Opera House? Such a relief to walk across the sweeping harbourside and to arrive at a finely balanced and generously invitational combination of structure and setting. Neither intimidating nor excessive. And, yes, well worth the wait. I had another space-inspiring book, this one about caving, *Ten Years Under the Earth*, by Norbert Casteret, black-and-white photographs and scary stories of the famous Frenchman's adventures down in the dark abyss of flooded grottoes. I still love buildings with a cave-like containment, volumes hollowed out of solid mass.

In my youth I'd not yet met with an actual living architect. From my father's succinct definition, I might have thought too literally about the idea of shape as outline, as if the architect's job was to drape the cape over the skeleton. Two externally unconnected but inwardly exciting developments helped educate my mind, began the turn towards a better understanding of architecture: a fortnight's stay at a Connemara holiday house in my mid-teenage years; and my father's subscription to a British monthly magazine, *Architectural Design*.

The Box, a house on its holidays, still extant and surviving intact, is the essence of the invisible house. Seen from the road, if it's noticed at all, it looks like an insignificant shed. Set down low on its sloping site, it interferes with no lines of sight across the rocky landscape. A closer look reveals that it stands on stubby piers, designed to straddle a seasonal stream. It avoids injury to the skyline and it hardly hits the ground. No windows to the timber-battened rear wall or in the solid brick sides. No walls, except the brick chimney, to interrupt the big windows to the sea. A simple plan, bunk rooms to the rear, to the roadside, an open plan living space (there's that 'space' word again) overhanging the land, overlooking the two beaches of our childhood holidays. We could view from on high the tents on Dog's Bay and caravans on Gurteen, two of the most spectacular beaches in the west of Ireland, with their white shelly sand and consequently turquoise seawater. Back-to-back beaches in a tombolo, like a sleeping couple turned away from each other, both heads resting on the sand-dune pillow of the headland. In the rocks at Gurteen I had found a place of my own, a seat-shaped shelf where you could sit with your back against the granite and gaze out to sea, getting a feeling for the elements of architecture. The spatial landscape of The Box offered something similar, the floor slab stepped down to encircle a fireplace, a proper 1960s conversation pit, a commonplace of international architecture at the time but an entirely novel discovery for me, perfect for ghost stories after dark. This jolt in level gives a jaunty look to the sea-facing elevation, except it's not easy to see this open face, either from below on the beach or from atop the distant headland. The design was widely credited at the time to the sculptor Gary Trimble. Years later, while working at the Office of Public Works, I met his widow, Joan, the modest and as yet uncredited architect-author of this more than modest building. The Box, a minor example of Albert Einstein's maxim 'as simple as possible but no simpler', opened my eyes to the idea of ideas in architecture, house as tent, house as cave, house that hovers, house as viewing device, house that hides itself from view, hiding below the immediate horizon to hold the view of the distant horizon, the entire borrowed landscape contained within itself. Lessons learned from early experience, drawn on for later experiments, tested by trial and error.

And the other thing, the second thing, was reading the *AD*, sifting through the growing pile of those magazines stacked outside the door of my father's office. There can't have been too many provincial engineers who subscribed to such a cutting-edge journal. I think my father must have done it to encourage my interest. My first taste of London's lively architecture scene and the first inkling of the intellectual possibility or social purpose of architectural practice came from thumbing the pages of *Architectural Design*. I read and re-read, without any real understanding, the densely crafted criticism of Kenneth Frampton, James Stirling's experimental buildings cunningly reviewed by Alvin Boyarsky, obscure marginalia written by Alison Smithson masquerading under the weird pseudonym I. Chippendale. When I found myself back in London after my student days, many of these distant figures emerged out of the pages of the *AD* to turn into actual real people, and, by my good fortune, some of them, especially Stirling, who gave me my first job in the basement of Gloucester Place; Boyarsky, who hosted our first exhibition in the basement of the Architectural Association in London; Frampton, whose writing informed our intellectual starting position, became patrons of a kind. Sometime champions, sympathetic allies always. Generous people, helpful mentors and critical friends, these London connections gifted me with some of the most significant forces of influence in my formation as an architect.

Dublin Dimensions

There are places I'll remember
All my life, though some have changed
John Lennon and Paul McCartney, 'In My Life'

IF BLACK AND WHITE had changed to colour with the move to Cooley, my world expanded into three dimensions as soon as I landed in the studios of the School of Architecture at University College Dublin. Within a month of the move from Dundalk to Dublin, I'd broken up with my girlfriend. Within a year I'd lost touch with any friend I'd had from the town. It was a time to start anew, to begin again with this new life in architecture. Cut off from schooldays, in the instant of awareness of the enlarged scope of what was promised, this newly expanded environment just as suddenly shrank down to fit my new surroundings, and step by step, slowly grew out again from there. Graham Greene wrote that there's always one moment in childhood when the door opens and lets the future in. That moment happened, that door opened for me, when I was seventeen and first stumbled into my future in architecture.

First year was spent down in the hessian-walled basement, moving up to ground floor for second and fourth years, second-floor student-built mezzanines for third and final years. Social life revolved around the lofty studios, big rooms with high windows, wooden drawing boards and trestle tables. The old university buildings at Earlsfort Terrace were wrapped around the volume of the Great Hall, later to become the National Concert Hall. From the upper studios, we could clamber up through narrow stairways and shimmy on our knees across the dark roof space of the Great Hall. We watched concerts by the Chieftains and Alan Stivell down through the ventilation grilles in the ceiling, squatting on our precarious perches, high up in the trusswork.

Most of the university community had begun the big move out to the new suburban campus in Belfield, leaving behind the faculties of architecture, medicine and parts of engineering in the palatial corridors and underpopulated spaces of Earlsfort Terrace. Medical students were across the yard; we had no contact with them. We shared a few maths lectures with the engineering students, but there was not much contact there either. In a strange way, moving from school at the Marist in Dundalk to the School of Architecture at UCD, was a move from one isolated community of two hundred students and staff to another. But the cultures were different. The questions were different. Now, in this new world, the world was opening up.

One early exposure for me to the bohemian depths of this newfound city happened at a basement folk club in Parnell Square, the memory still vivid. A boy, maybe fifteen, certainly younger than my seventeen years, was sitting in the corner with a guitar. People gathered around to hear him sing and play. He was singing something so incredible in its raw intensity and mysterious vision I was amazed, intimidated. How could one so young have come up with such a song, when I, being so much older, had achieved nothing to compare? 'I put my fingers against the glass and bowed my head and cried.' Later, to my embarrassment, but really to my relief, I came to realise that while the performance was his own, the song, 'I Dreamed I Saw St Augustine', belonged to Bob Dylan, who had changed the whole world by the time he was twenty-two. I still had those five years ahead of me, or so I consoled myself, plenty of time yet. 'Ah, but I was so much older then, I'm younger than that now.'

You could escape the confines of the studio, all worldly confines in fact, by slipping across the street to the Irish Film Theatre, perfectly placed for afternoon disappearances. Bergman's *The Silence* was among the first of many miserable things I enjoyed seeing there. In the evenings we went to the Astor on the Quays, to relish further gloomy doses of Bergman, the blood-red crisis of *Cries and Whispers*, but other more romantic distractions too. I don't know what my visual education would have been without the impact and influence of cinema. In our later student years my fellow student Sheila and I used to cycle out to Belfield for Film Society screenings, the whispering complexity of *Spirit of the Beehive*, the magnificence of *The Seven Samurai*, the erotic work ethic of *Woman in the Dunes* and many other masterworks bringing us closer together in the darkened lecture room. When I say we used to cycle, I mean to say she travelled on the crossbar of my bike, and this clever move brought us even closer than the movies. We've lived together closely now for forty-seven years.

The Coffee Inn on South Anne Street was an unpretentious place, perfectly suited to students with little money and cosmopolitan pretensions. It served hard-baked pizzas on small plates and milky cappuccinos in translucent white cups, a night-time cheap café that brought you to some other city, the promise of somewhere far away, Italy. By contrast, for lunch, the Country Shop, not far down Stephen's Green from the torch-carrying Nubian princesses of the Shelbourne Hotel, but far removed from their splendour, its modest sign a thatched cottage swinging from the railings. A cosy, welcoming place, pleasantly run by the probably conservative Irish Countrywomen's Association, where, in a top-lit inner room, cushioned against the outside world, macaroni cheese was served in small oval brown and yellow earthenware dishes.

For daytime distraction there were three Bewley's cafés; Grafton Street as the pivotal hub, Westmoreland Street for fireside chats and George's Street to really escape the crowd. One defining aspect of this Quaker-run café was that money never changed hands in the big room, an honour system inherent to the culture of the 'clattery café'. You told them on the way out what you'd had, paying up at a little cashier's box in the front shop. You could spend a lot of time and relatively little money in Bewley's. The place was full of thrifty people savouring solitary almond buns selected from the triple-stacked trays of treats on every table, ordering more hot water for their pots of tea, reading books and writing letters. Hours went by without interruption, especially if you'd bagged a seat in one of the high-backed red velvet banquettes. You could be broke and yet be comfortable, at your ease in the elegant corners of this down-at-heel town, being broke very different from being poor. Flats were cheap to rent, money didn't talk so loud.

In another time, years later, walking down George's Street with a visiting client from the Derry-based community language organisation An Gaeláras, a man of my age, he stopped across the street from the café to ask, 'What's Bewley's?' I set it all out for him, our student haven, an exclusive club without membership, a place apart for those with time on their hands, no longer in existence now, not as it was. Why did he ask? 'Oh, just because when we were all on the blanket above in the H Blocks, we used to wonder to ourselves, "What's Bewley's?"'

One of the big dilemmas of our time, for our student generation, insulated as we were from the street politics and realities of what was going on in the North, rose from the stifling control that the Catholic Church held over our intellectual education, and, by extension, for some at least, this provoked the wider question of the very idea of a deity. For those so afflicted, symptoms of this disease surfaced as an existential struggle in the late teens and early twenties, and it would have been the topic of intense discussions over tea in Bewley's, over pints in Hartigan's, in bedsits and on buses. The God question had to be got rid of, got away out of the way, once and for all, before human life could continue its course. The existentialist proposition, as much as it was understood to affect us in real life, was to envisage each person as responsible for their own decisions and, as a consequence, the multiple accumulation of conscious choices would result in the formation of the person. The novels of Jean-Paul Sartre and Simone de Beauvoir were widely read in these times, their philosophical writings rarely referred to, apart from *The Second Sex*, and while such predicaments were probably already out of date in much of the rest of Europe, they were crucial in the student culture of my university days. The next critical question, and closely connected, was introduced via the feminist movement, arrived in the air, as if fresh from abroad, in our second year, bringing with it the liberating realisation that gender equality could exert a practical influence of benefit to your personal foundation. We had substituted religion for a vaguely humanistic dose of atheism and now, irregular readers of the monthly *Spare Rib*, with female consciousness raised and male consciences questioned, we struggled to overcome our limitations and tried to reimagine ourselves as free-thinking individuals.

This kind of talk had already begun to cause trouble at home in Dundalk by the end of my schooldays. Rows and ructions with my mother, petty clashes with the clergy, ripples in the still pond of family life. All of which, during my first year in Dublin, led to an unpleasant appointment with my father, of all people, in Bewley's, of all places. It was not a good meeting. He handed me a folded piece of paper, written out in his own elegant engineer's fountain pen cursive script, citing chapter and verse, Matthew 18.6. I was close enough to my Catholic training to recognise the biblical warning to those risking the downfall of the little ones: 'it would be better for him to have a great millstone hung around the neck and to be drowned in the depths of the sea'. He told me straight I would not be welcome to visit the family home, not unless I shut up about such matters while I was there. Drowned in the depths of the sea. What a thing to say. His own father was drowned in the sea. He himself had nearly drowned in the sea when he was in the Navy. He had helped me one time with a school essay for English class, the given title being 'The Cruel Sea'. At the time, I would have been unaware of Nicholas Monsarrat's novel of the same name, a survival story about Navy men, their life aboard ship and their clashes with

German torpedoes, later made into a movie. So I could not have been conscious of its close parallels with my father's wartime experience, events scarcely referred to in my childhood days. I had started my essay with a short passage about the ancient Greeks offering victims to appease the gods, to which he suggested the addition of a well-worded phrase – 'They were wasting their time flinging them in, the sea being indifferent to human sacrifice.' Now, here, in the room where money wasn't mentioned, he had named his price. I got angry and told him so. 'Shame on you,' I said. He said little in defence. Once before, in my teenage years, I had voiced my doubts on one of our days out fly fishing on the River Fane. He told me that we both knew it was mumbo jumbo, but best go through the motions and keep such thoughts to myself. At the time, this shared scepticism had been a great help to my schoolboy survival. But the Bewley's diktat, delivered inside the crucible of independent life in the city, smacked of something much less companionable and I didn't like it, didn't expect it, not from him. Both of us ashamed, uncomfortable, out of our depth, we stared it out over coffee and buns.

He redeemed himself soon after my first student summer in London. I had saved some money working as a street sweeper in the last season of the Covent Garden Market, and headed off on an Interrail ticket to Athens, at the end of the train line covered by the ticket. Arriving back in Dublin, a little late for the start of college term, I found that my parents had taken the precaution of booking me into Hatch Hall, a Jesuit-run student residence, the same place I'd been unhappily installed in my first year. I was determined to rent a flat, ready to pay my way with savings from all those summer jobs. After a few days, having found a flat, I told the principal at the student residence that I was moving out. Priestly fury rained down on me; he refused to countenance any such wilful intentions. I rang my father, beginning to set out my predicament, stupidly unaware that he'd already paid for my bed and board, knowing nothing of his own financial straits at the time. He interrupted, just the once, to ask if there was a back door. Yes, I knew a door from the kitchen out onto the back lane. 'Then pack your bag and use it,' he said. And he sought no further explanation, never mentioned it again. Freedom regained; trust reinstated.

That first flat, along the grand cliff face of Pembroke Road, a short-term stay before transferring across the canal to a second-floor bedsit on the still finer cliff face of Leeson Street, might have been an ex-brothel, judging by grateful messages scrawled on the wallpaper. The cramped conditions of Parson's canal bridge bookshop made a civilised stopping point on the cycle into college, conveniently located between Pembroke Road and Earlsfort Terrace. It was to become a regular haunt, a safe house where I bought a very few books and read many more in between the book stacks, all under the hospitable gaze of two genteel ladies who seemed perfectly at ease with their shop being treated as a library. Paul Klee's slim but cryptic essay *On Modern Art* was one of my first Parson's purchases, still on my shelves, an inspirational invitation to think about thinking about drawing. Nearby, in the other direction, the cosy hideout of the Carnegie Library had a heavy volume on the complete works of Paul Klee. And the capacious Architecture Library at Earlsfort Terrace had a pristine copy of his *Thinking Eye*. I went through a period of immersion in Klee, impressed by his drawings, awed by his multiple capabilities, mystified by the often-mystical obscurity of his writings. At the simplest level, I learned to draw lines for measure before venturing into tone or colour, to follow his direction to take the line for a walk and other life lessons in draughtsmanship.

The Leeson Street flat was situated brilliantly close to our studios in Earlsfort Terrace, a social centre for student shenanigans, with the IFT cinema and Hartigan's pub halfway in between. Late-night sessions in the Leeson Street flat. Coffee-seeking students drifting by on their way home from town often came to stay, often staying longer than intended. A law student, with the fine voice of a future senior counsel, used to boom my name from a standing position in the middle of the empty street canyon, hands cupped around his mouth, a night owl in the early hours – 'Jo-ho-ohn Tu-hoo-omey!' – until I dropped the key down onto the granite pavement. The people from the upstairs flat called down one night to borrow my guitar. There was a guy with them, they said, who would be worth hearing if I wanted to come up. Whoever he was, that blues guitarist – I never found out his name – turned out to be quite brilliant. In his fluent hands and under his fast fingers, my Yamaha FG-140 steel-stringed guitar played like a different instrument entirely. I felt betrayed, couldn't ever look at the guitar in the same way again; it had never sounded like that for me.

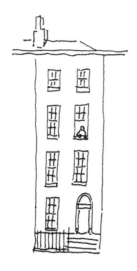

One Saturday morning the landlord, an old military man known as the Colonel, called in the usual way for his £4 weekly rent. But this time the poor man seemed disturbed, scandalised even, asking whether it was true what he'd been told, that we'd had women staying over in the flat. He hauled us down to the communal bathroom on the half-landing, pointing with dismay to an enormous padded bra jammed down the toilet. We denied any connection with this crime against decency. Anyway, how could he think we'd have anything to do with anything like that? All the women we knew had burned their bras by the end of their time in first year.

It wasn't until those early days of my second year at UCD that I managed to overcome an inherent or shy apprehension and head in to Mrs Gaj's restaurant. There were times in the first year when I'd hung around the corner of Baggot Street, lingering beneath the first floor windows, waiting for permission or for some initiation rite to allow me to enter, sometimes venturing up the stairs to peer through the steamed-up glass door. The evening I finally made it through that door to the warm interior, so easy and inviting, it was a wonder that it had taken so long to break through the barriers and step inside. Any impediment had been on my side, but admission having been earned the hard way, I felt I belonged, like a pilgrim arrived at his own micro mecca. 'All the best spies eat at Gaj's,' said the ad in *Hibernia*. For the rest of my time in college this place became central HQ of many social and political operations. In Dundalk there'd been a café I'd never felt cool enough to enter, the Espresso, down a dark lane off Park Street. I thought it was reserved for those who had paid their dues, could play the blues, who knew the news. I was not sure who they were. I was not among them. The closest I'd come to a haunt in Dundalk was the Afton Club, 'th'Afton', where we had danced around under dandruff-illuminating, white bra-revealing black–purple disco lights.

Access to the Afton was down another of Park Street's side lanes, across a bridge over the canalised Rampart River, symbolically situated outside town limits, but still close to the centre. Very different from the Adelphi Ballroom, directly attached to the back of the cinema, where the showbands played, and where we never ventured. 'Flow gently sweet Afton' was printed on every pack of Carroll's *Sweet Afton* cigarettes made in Dundalk. Across the Ramparts we would flow, to meet at the Afton, a low-lying, roadside corrugated shed. A black-floored, dark-walled interior with a small bar serving Coke and Fanta, and a shadier space behind, best placed, probably, for a shift against the back wall, but not for me. I'd be stationed up close to the stage, admiring the band, beat bands like Skid Row and Granny's Intentions. If you wanted to get a dance with a girl, having eyed her up from a distance, you had to cross the valley floor to where the girls were lined up, huddled together on the opposite bench. Go over and ask her up, reach out your hand, risking the chance of refusal – 'Sorry, I'm with my friends.' Smokers seemed to be at an advantage in this game. Stubbing out a dropped cigarette on the floor acted like an initial dance step, synchronised with a sudden and decisive advance towards the prey. How could I match this manouevre? Cleaning your glasses on the tail of your shirt wouldn't cut the mustard. Side by side after a slow set, holding hands now, if you were lucky, you'd be waiting for the secret sign of a bent finger scratching into the palm of your hand, meaning you can walk me home. Speaking of luck, one late night/early morning, walking one particular girl home down by the Ramparts, we'd seen the flash of a kingfisher dipping close to the water. One night only.

But now, upstairs, ensconced in Gaj's, I could breathe easy. Several times a week, after lectures or before the cinema,

I sat down at a square wooden table to French toast, bacon and pineapple or goulash with rice. One time my parents came to visit, the Leeson Street bedsit not being the setting for such an occasion, I thought I'd risk bringing them to Gaj's. The unapproachable blonde waitress quietly approached, asked whether these were my parents and ushered us over to sit at Mrs Gaj's table. The corner table, where plots were hatched, kindly proffered for parental entertainment. I'd found my place, on the inside with the outsiders.

In my third year, I was elected auditor of ArcSoc, the student architectural society at UCD. I had fallen into fellowship with an activist crowd from the College of Art, then located in nearby Kildare Street. They were in dispute with the establishment concerning what is art and how it ought to be taught. It was decided that we should occupy the college, art and architecture students acting in solidarity. The College of Art was adjacent to the National Library, where I had come by a reader's ticket to access Hegel's lectures on aesthetics, unobtainable in the UCD library at the time. Hegelian theories have long sunk out of any conscious recollection. But, because of this reading, I knew my way to the college door. We planned to rush in late in the evening, just as the porters were closing the doors. It turned out that trouble was expected, with a wall of guards ready to hold the gate. What were we to do? 'Put your head down and run between their legs!' said my friend from the art college. This I knew how to do from my days back in the after-mass rush in Grange. Once inside, we realised we had no food, no preparations and no intention of giving up. The occupation went on for a few days, maybe five, and it was a tremendous success. Puppet shows, pretend wrestling contests, pseudo art crits, falling asleep on the floor to *The Dark Side of the Moon*. I can't say whether the social dynamic of this event sparked any particular change of policy in art education, although it might have provided the push that was needed, but I do know that friendships were formed that have lasted a lifetime.

I was a serious-minded student, immature and under-skilled when I started out at UCD, distracted by everything around me, student politics included, but keen to learn and thrilled by the thought of a purposeful life in architecture. I loved being in the studio. Through my college years I lived off the energy inspired by my experience in the first year. At the end of term assessment meeting, one tutor, the one who mattered, leant over across the table and told me, confidentially, as if convinced he could see into the faraway future, 'You have the makings of a great architect!' I don't know whether this was something he might have said to others, I'm sure it wasn't merited by the work in my portfolio, but, at this stage, early in my studies, it hit me hard, struck me by surprise, a boost that gave me strength to survive the difficult seasons ahead. Later, in my third year, a different tutor told me, 'You're a funny fellow, you think too much, and you don't do enough work!' There was a truth in this assertion that I couldn't deny.

Dabbling in student activism nearly got me into trouble on a day the university's president arrived with the

Minister for Education, to take a walking tour of Earlsfort Terrace. A protest was hastily arranged. As the minister made to leave, a group of students gathered around his car, intending to block any easy exit. We began to rock the vehicle, gently, no plan to do harm, but it wouldn't have seemed friendly if you were inside the car. The president, in the heat of the moment, intervened in the fray. I yelled something unseemly. He pulled me away from the car. Grabbed me fiercely by the wrists. He was a rough enough character and threatening in his bulk. We were staring eye to eye. It seemed that serious repercussions would be in store. Just then, a lanky student, in a gallant gesture, sprang up on the bonnet of the ministerial car and, pointing down at our little scuffle, shouted in an assumed voice of urgent authority, 'Take your hands off him! He's our representative!' This was a surprisingly effective ruse. It defused the moment. The monster relaxed his grip. And, in the commotion, I got lost among the crowd. And got away with it again.

Another influential occupation happened in my final year, to more measurably practical effect: the Pembroke Street protest. One night in Hartigan's, early in January 1976, after a meal in Gaj's, we decided to go over the wall at the back of five Georgian houses where covert demolition had begun in the lull after Christmas. There was a guard dog just inside the wall. I began to back off in fear of this big black animal, but the guy beside me, a student from the other school, the Bolton Street College of Technology, murmured, 'It's alright, I'm a dog handler.' That dog turned out to be our mascot for the months of the sit-in. Bord na Móna, moving on to new offices, had declared these fine old buildings to be in unsound condition and had offered the site for sale for office development. Planning permission to demolish had been refused, but this decision was overturned by ministerial order, and action was taken to begin work while no one was looking. We went in with no advance plans made, except to do something to stop the demolition, and stayed for thirteen weeks. Eventually up to seventy architecture students, from Dublin's two schools of architecture, were in occupation on a rota, a few nights on and off in turn. We played darts and held tournaments in the hallway, the dartboard hanging dangerously on the back of the front door. A mass meeting was smoothly chaired by the Arts Council director. Useful guidance was offered by the director of the National Gallery, advising that any negotiations should end with a communiqué, which would be best written in advance. Politicians stopped by with words of support. The first-floor connecting rooms were surveyed, measured drawings were made, and the piano nobile was suitably renamed the Syd Barrett Memorial Suite. Food would sometimes be sent up from Gaj's to keep us going. Sheila and I were supposed to be doing our theses, which were now neglected for much of the time. We got together amid all the excitement. We're still together, the demolition was stopped, the houses survive and perhaps the occupation helped call a halt to an insidious trend of Georgian demolition and façade retention. Nowadays, walking down Pembroke Street, we still feel a sense of ownership over one particular kink in Dublin's brick streetscape. We've built the geometry of that angled bend into more than one of our buildings.

Despite these distractions, my thesis got done. Or almost done, enough done to get me out of college. The scheme was regarded by professor and examiners as undeveloped beyond its outline idea. But I probably meant it to be sparse and outline. I wanted a communicative building, a newspaper office, a radical design rising out of a sharply triangular site, broken into blocks and cylinders of translucent glass and structural steel, with information screens at different levels to address a public podium plaza and to broadcast news events down the axis of O'Connell Street. I wanted it skin and bones, elemental. It might have seemed diagrammatic to those who wanted more detail, but it's the only design I made in college that matters to the work I do now. I decorated my drawings with pencil-shaded likenesses of Fernand Léger's long-haired ladies. When, finally, I got to see the flashing liquid lights of Times Square, with the latest plasma screen technology – non-existent in 1976 – I found the experience unsympathetic in the extreme. Too much colour, much too intrusive on the shape of the city. I thought to myself, like the little woman in the nursery rhyme running home from the market, 'This is none of I.' My student vision for a public information display had been imagined as monochrome images projected in layered transparencies, fleeting lines and shimmering shadows in black and white and grey. Be careful what you wish for.

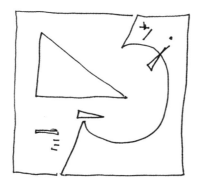

My library reading was a steady diet of Russian Constructivism (hence the politically driven choice of newspaper office as propaganda machine), early Le Corbusier, Louis Kahn, British Brutalism. But the strictness of this twentieth-century regime could be tempered by the odd surprise distraction discovered between the usual books along the shelves. This way, browsing along Dewey Decimal class 724, seeking out another publication on the Vesnin brothers' *Pravda* newspaper building or Jan Duiker's Open Air School, you could plunge headlong unawares into the nineteenth century. On the library shelves, there lurked a purple velvet-bound volume on the works of William Burges, a book that smacked of decadence, at odds with my puritanical student tendencies. Burges designed everything – wallpaper, cutlery, furniture, everything. It is rumoured that he hadn't visited the site when he designed St Fin Barre's Cathedral, surely the finest building in Cork, and most convincingly integrated into its urban landscape.

Perhaps he didn't need a site visit; he was busy measuring every gothic cathedral in France and maybe that was all the inspiration he needed for the job. He won the project at competition in 1862, at the age of thirty-five. I learned recently that his diary entry on the day of the big win simply reads 'Got Cork'. And so he did, Burges really got Cork. And young Jørn Utzon, likewise, got Sydney. Just like Burges, in his mid-thirties he won the Sydney Opera House competition without ever setting foot on the site, and went on to create a civic masterwork belonging to its place. Utzon relied on nautical maps to understand from afar the spectacular topography of Sydney Harbour. Cork's hilly streetscape, only a little less spectacular, luxuriously sprawls across its sandstone contours, in mocking contrast to Dublin's undeniably fair, but essentially flat, city.

By such serendipity, fishing in the library shelves, I came across Viollet-le-Duc's *The Habitations of Man in All Ages*, a strange volume on the origins of domestic architecture. Doxius and his companion Epergos – yes, those are their preposterous names – wander the world to discover and describe different tribal settlements. One elegant phrase still lingers from my lazy days dipping into Viollet-le-Duc's flowery prose, where Doxius attempts to preach to the Peruvian people: 'They listened or appeared to listen to him, but his words glided from their minds like water on polished marble.'

Midway through my studies, my father had given me an Everyman edition of John Ruskin's *Seven Lamps of Architecture*, seven essays on social philosophy and aesthetic morality, first published in 1849. Even from the distance of more than a century, although Victorian in its values and convoluted in its language, his writing made an impact on me, still does today. His *Stones of Venice* opened my eyes to the layered surfaces of the Venetian Gothic. On one of my schoolboy outings, my father had brought me to see the geology department's Museum Building in Trinity College, the Deane and Woodward building that Ruskin had declared the finest building in Europe. My father had completed his post-war engineering studies in Trinity College, and his lectures had been held in that building. He walked me around the perimeter of the florid box to explain how each of the stone-sculpted bosses, flower-based decorations carved by the O'Shea brothers, craftsmen from Cork, varied one from another, similar in type but otherwise not repetitive in design. Much later I learned that Ruskin had refused the RIBA Royal Gold Medal, explaining his refusal by citing four examples of architectural neglect or destruction: two crumbling churches in Florence; the altarpiece of another in Pisa; and the ruins of Furness Abbey, newly threatened by vibrations from passing trains. Shocked by 'the sacrifice of any and all to temporary convenience', he felt he had no option other than to decline. In an era of such emergencies, he declared, 'it is no time for us to play at adjudging medals to each other', an architect teetering on the territory of his moral high ground. The sin of pride, there it goes again.

Maurice Craig, in an account of writing his still indispensable book about the origins of the Georgian city, *Dublin, 1660–1860: The Shaping of a City*, recalled walking through Dublin in the early 1950s, never having to suffer the smell of newly sawn timber. Despite the destruction of the 1960s, it still felt that way in the early 1970s, melancholy, static. A changeless continuity seemed to have spread itself evenly across the walkable city, from Parson's to Gaj's, from Bewley's to the bottles-only Brazen Head. It was high time for a change, we were hungry for change, change was long overdue and badly needed, and change was surely coming – but the slow-time stability of Dublin's urban environment, its hard-angled street corners, its quiet back lanes, the enveloping intimacy of its low-scaled street architecture, forms a scenographic back-projection that registers more clearly in reminiscence, a painterly presence that fixes the frame of my rear-view vision and shapes the image of the city of my student years.

In and Out of London

Posted, eyes front, along the dreamy ramparts
Of escalators ascending and descending
To a monotonous slight rocking in the works,
We were moved along, upstanding.

Seamus Heaney, 'District and Circle'

MY FATHER TOOK ME on one final one-to-one trip, the last of our solo outings together, in the spring of the year I'd left home for university. An eighteenth birthday treat must have been the excuse, but the stated purpose was to see the *Treasures of Tutankhamun*, a huge exhibition just opened at the British Museum. I'd never been to London; he hadn't been back since his honeymoon in the early 1950s. We stayed at the Regent Palace; an ocean liner of a hotel moored nose-in to the lights of Piccadilly Circus. His idea of eating out in London would have been places like the long-gone Lyons Corner House. I don't remember anything about where we ate. Nowhere special, I can be sure of that. We queued a long way around the block to get into the British Museum, then solemnly queued our way around inside the crowded labyrinth of the exhibition itself. It was a wonder, the golden mask shining out of the dark. He brought me up into the dome of St Paul's to experience the further wonder of the Whispering Gallery. We went to see the hippie musical *Hair* at the

Shaftesbury Theatre, calmly waiting with everybody else in the audience to register the mild shock of the notorious all-nude line-up and then, after the interval, settled down to enjoy the rest of the singalong show. We went to see the more notorious film, Stanley Kubrick's *A Clockwork Orange*, at the Warner West End in Leicester Square, the only cinema where it could be seen that year. This disturbingly unpleasant film was a challenging test of our unpractised liberality. Many left the movie midway. We sat through and survived it together.

The Shaftesbury Theatre was forced to close the following year, and the original Broadway production of *Hair* met an untimely end when part of the ceiling collapsed into the main auditorium. By a curious coincidence, *The Curious Incident of the Dog in the Night-time*, a West End play I saw much more recently on a rare London outing with my mother, met a similar end when the ceiling of the Apollo Theatre, also on Shaftesbury Avenue, fell down on the audience, injuring a few people sitting in the very seats where we'd been sitting, just one week after we saw the show. Despite these practical proofs of the necessary co-dependence of architecture and engineering, between shaping space and calculating structure, with no objective connections between these two closed shows, I hold on to my personal connections with the experience of encirclement embodied in these horseshoe-shaped auditoria.

I don't remember anything of what my father and I talked about during those few days in London.

Conversation was never his strong point, although always a good man to tell a story when the occasion demanded. We were on an adventure, two men together, building a bridge across the generation gap, out in the city to broaden our minds. It marked a moment of transition, home-leaving in the company of my father. And it was my introduction to London, the streets of London, the gloomy hills of London, the London which was to become a recurring fixture of my background for the next ten years.

I set out again for London that first student summer with an old friend from school. We thought we had well-paid jobs fixed up for ourselves, our confidence unreliably based on the strength of one phone call and the open offer of work made a few short weeks before our departure. We turned up as planned, early on a Monday morning, tired off the boat train, at a little fish-dyeing works, a small place stacked full of sides of salmon hanging from its smoky ceiling, just opposite Chalk Farm tube station, only to be told those jobs were long gone, they couldn't be waiting around for two boys to sail in from Ireland.

And so began a summer of casual work, with serial glimpses gained into the ordinary underworld workings of the city. We moved into a cheap hostel in a once-grand house on Norland Square in Holland Park. My schoolfriend got called back home to study for repeat exams, my last contact with schooldays gone. I was to spend the rest of the summer on my own. My first outing was to the Electric Cinema Club on Portobello Road. I bought an army surplus jacket and sat around with blissed-out people in Ladbroke Grove, listening to Van Morrison's new album *Saint Dominic's Preview*, failing to find the sweet spot the others said they got from sucking dope smoke through long pasta straws fixed into screwtop bottle caps, 'trying hard to make this whole thing blend'. I was broke and needed work to keep me going. An ad in the *Evening Standard* promised to solve my immediate problem – 'Students Students Students!!! Money Money Money!!!'

After three days' brainwashing in Tottenham Court Road, with passports surrendered, not deemed to be trained until tested that the script had been properly memorised word for word, having learned my lines by reciting them out loud during evenings pacing about in Shepherd's Bush Green, small hunting parties were sent out in convoys around the suburbs to 'make placements' – in plain truth, to sell encyclopaedias. Knock on doors, we were told, say it's a sociological survey, ask for an appointment with Mr and Mrs Jones, tell them you'll be back later that evening. They must be both together and no one must leave the room. If anyone does leave the room you pack up and walk out of that house on the spot. Make up to five of these forty-minute pitches with no deviation from the transcript and you might expect two or even three 'placements' on a good night's fishing. Easy does it. Then wait in the local phone box you'd been dropped at for the van ride back into the city.

Having tricked my first victim into signing the papers, sealing the envelope and storing it away safely out of sight on a high shelf, where the script told us it would likely be forgotten before the five-day cancellation date, I phoned in with my success to win the £38 prize for the first hit of the night. I felt filthy with guilt. I'd proved I could do it easily enough, but I couldn't be easy doing it. It took a week's persuasion to extract my passport from the safe of the sun-tanned crook who swore I was passing up on the chance to fly my own helicopter by the time I was twenty-five. Apparently, we'd all been signed up for a month, otherwise our training would have to be counted as a wasted investment. I worked my way through Mario Puzo's *The Godfather*, hunched down on the floors of suburban telephone boxes; it got me through my unhappy week as an inactive door-to-door salesman. With no further earnings, having made no further placements, with £11 docked from my first night's winnings for wear and tear to the plastic briefcase handed out on the first day, I escaped the gangster life.

Two weeks into London life I was running out of money, living on a tin of beans a day. Unsuccessful in the early-morning line-ups outside Chalk Farm Tube station, standing with the big men waiting for building-site work, I never once got picked to jump up on the back of a truck, never got a start. Trusted as a new-found friend by young Egyptian roommates in the hostel, accepted on the shaky basis of having seen the mask of Tutankhamun, they told me I should do what they did; go to Earl's Court before six in the morning and sign on for day-to-day hire with Industria Personnel Services.

I'd have to buy an alarm clock to wake up in time for the job hunt. I spent the last of my money on one of those round-faced wind-up contraptions, with glow-in-the-dark numerals and twin bells on top. Running for the Tube, I stretched out my hand to hold the departing train, expecting the doors would re-open automatically and I could hop aboard. My hand, holding the clock, got jammed in the closing doors. And the train started. 'Drop the clock!' they yelled from inside the train. I didn't want to let go, trotting alongside the moving train, my hand inside, not giving up. Not thinking ahead to the approaching tunnel. Not realising the danger. 'Drop the clock!' Somehow, suddenly, the doors opened and we both survived, my new clock and me. I was reminded of that early near miss by a recent mishap in the now-familiar stop at Holborn Underground station, changing trains from the Piccadilly line to the Central line on the way out to site at Stratford. I was last to leave the carriage, the last carriage on the train, at the end of the curving platform, out of sight of the driver's rear-view mirror, 'Mind the Gap' written large on the platform, the gap between the straight edge of the train and the bend in the shape of the station. I leaned out to step over, bags in hand, when the doors closed on my neck. It must have been a comical sight, my head held outside the sleek carriage, clamped in a trap, body wriggling within. Then the engine started. People shouting and banging on the side of the train had its effect, and eventually those doors slid open, I stumbled out and the train moved on. Escaped with no worse than a rubber-blackened ring above my shirt collar. Fifty years between these two escapes, minor events in the everyday life of the Underground, either one of them might have been major for me. But, in both cases, lucky for me, lucky me, I got away with these what-if brushes with mortality, my own *Sliding Doors* moments.

The wonder of those first days down in the Underground, a warm and rumbling world apart, rambling around beneath the city, wooden slatted escalators sinking and rising, endless spiral stairs, throughway lifts with indicator lights, intersecting passageways echoing to buskers performing, the cosmopolitan comfort of it all. The below-ground infrastructure of the Underground. Easy to locate entrances to the labyrinth, handy to find at a street corner like Chalk Farm, with its oxblood terracotta-tiled arches. Fifty of these distinctive red stations were designed in two years by a man named Green, a few more years before the bar and circle logo consolidated the image of the Tube. To a new arrival in London, familiar in advance with its urban form from one year's discovery of Dublin, a much smaller but somewhat similar metropolis, being a capital city made up of houses, repetitive rows of brick houses, street façades measured out simply by the span of available timber joists, it was thrilling to disappear off the map in one place and to emerge in a faraway extension of the same street system. To pop up with no sense of orientation in an until-now unknown Earl's Court, Cannon Street or back at the original landing place of Chalk Farm, the first place I surfaced after the mailboat train brought me into Euston, later to become my home station for the final few years of living and working in London.

The first night's casual labour was cleaning the kitchens in the Savoy Hotel. As a new recruit, I was assigned the ceiling extract ductwork. The trick was to crawl along inside the duct as far as you could, pushing a bucket of caustic solution in front of you, painting your way backwards to the point of entry, scrubbing and sponging the grease off four sides of the narrow tunnel, all the while holding your breath. It was a grimily gruesome task. Walking home exhausted from the Savoy towards Holland Park, a white Rolls Royce loomed out of the dark at Marble Arch and offered me a lift. I climbed high up into the front seat. The back seat passenger seemed very interested to hear all about my night's work, and as we stopped outside a Bayswater hotel, having heard me out, he told the driver to take me on home to my Holland Park hostel. I had wrongly assumed the driver was the owner, but the friendly bloke in the back turned out to be Joe Cocker. 'Oh, I get by with a little help from my friends.'

My next job was in an East London gin factory, rolling barrels through the bare-earth-floored warehouse so that the customs and excise man could test the alcohol content, sucking up small samples from each cask in a pipette, his job not mine.

Then a few days in the Hudson's Bay Company, a fur trading business located in the appropriately named Beaver House near Skinners Lane. Viewed from afar, the City of London appears as a cluster of high buildings huddled at random. Closer in and you realise these new buildings are rising out of old ground, that the city is a labyrinth of lanes and passageways. Here, deep inside the city street network, I learned to sort astrakhan hides by their relative curliness, five grades from rough to smooth, bound in bundles by the neck and stacked high on wide wooden trestles. The Asian man I worked under took the easy way to stay sociable by calling everybody around him Jim. He boasted all day about sex – 'Twice last night with wife, Jim!' – 'You scratch my back, I scratch your bollocks, Jim!' He was respected as the astrakhan expert, running his fingers softly over the rippled lambswool surface, eyes half-closed, never doubting his feel, subdividing those skins into their five categories. At lunch break you could walk through the low-ceilinged spaces of the warehouse, rooms hung with silver fox, brushing your face against silky furs from all around the world.

Then another few days at the Metal Box Factory, the noisiest place I've ever been. All day long, cans rattled along rail tracks crisscrossing in the air overhead, an amalgam of automated production and repetitive hard labour, ear-crashing racket and soul-crushing work. My task was simple: pressure-testing closed cans in tanks of cold water, a rudimentary process, any tedium relieved by alternating the arm that plunged the tin and the foot that drove the pedal. Most mornings, one of the lines of machinery would stall and we would sit it out for a cup of tea while the mechanics fixed the breakdown, separate tea rooms for men and women. The old men compared life now with a better life during the war. One big man, enquiring about my Kerry roots, told me he still read *The Kerryman* every week, although he hadn't been back to the Kingdom in thirty years. He seemed to be suffering from the worst kind of homesickness, the kind that can't be cured by going home.

Later in the afternoons, to make up for lost time, the lines would gradually build up speed, running faster like they do in the accelerated scenes from Charlie Chaplin's *Modern Times*, just as hectic as in the silent movie, but here in surround-sound and noisy beyond belief. Recently, in the Tate Modern, I saw an early 1970s archive film made in the Metal Box Factory, and was reminded of the deadened faces of the women working on the production line, sitting all day beside their cardboard boxes full of tin discs, loosely placing a pre-pressed lid on every passing can, lids ready to be hammered home further along the line, the pace of work in this bedlam at the mercy of the men who controlled the machine.

And so it went on, day after day, waiting to be picked at random, one of a gang piling in to fill a van, setting out from Earl's Court early in the morning, off to some unknown destination to help out for one day, three days, or, if you were lucky, a week to get used to the work.

Until someone told me of a chance as a street sweeper in Covent Garden Market. Looking back, I see how lucky I was to witness the end of a deeply ingrained way of life there, the downtown market in its final year, the vegetable stalls and their stripe-suited vendors, the hustle and bustle of an urban tradition unique to London, the unique city. The day began with picking up your

barrow and brush from the Drury Lane depot, then a
few intense hours of heavy work, shovelling heaps of fruit
and vegetable waste, all this smelly stuff packed into the
mashing mouth of a rubbish truck. I worked with an old
man named Alf, a cockney gent, loved by the faded ladies
he kept flowers for every day, red gladioli salvaged from
the rubbish piles. 'You sweep over thar, an' Oi'll sweep
over 'ere,' he'd say in the lull after the morning rush, a
roll-your-own cigarette loosely attached to his projecting
lower lip, the smouldering butt migrating from side
to side, moving across his mouth of its own accord.
Afternoons were whiled away at this more leisurely pace,
trundling the now-lighter wooden barrow down now-
quiet lanes, sweeping up here and there, stopping to
read on a bench in the little park behind Inigo Jones's
wide-eaved barn. This was the market life cycle captured
so clearly in Hitchcock's crazed movie *Frenzy*, released
in that same summer of 1972, the last summer of the
Covent Garden Market.

The Photographers' Gallery had opened in Soho
the year before, based in a black-tiled building on Great
Newport Street. It was one of the few public places I felt
I could drop in wearing my working clothes, passing its
door on my way home from work, convenient to Leicester
Square on the Northern line. John Berger's *Ways of Seeing*
was published that same year – a book that taught us how
to look at images, at photographs and paintings, with a
critical eye. And the Photographers' Gallery was a place
where you could see, at first hand, such images presented

in a critical way. Later, in our working life, Sheila and I would work with the gallery to make its move to the other side of Soho. It would be our first building in London. But, for then, for me, it was one of my safe places in that big city.

That first summer in London, spent mostly alone, living from day to day, with the welcome relief and relative security of a regular job sweeping the cobbled streets, lives large in my memory.

It ended with a month's escape into the wider world, an Interrail journey across Europe from Paris to Athens, the first year of that under-21 travel pass on European railways, my first glimpse of the waterways of Venice, the walled cities of Split and Dubrovnik, camping on the coast of Croatia, meeting half my class from UCD in a hostel in Athens, ending up sleeping on empty beaches on the undiscovered island of Paros. The dream of a borderless Europe. On the way back my money ran low, but I was untroubled. I'd heard at the Athens hostel of an easy scam. Everybody's doing it, I was told. Just go to the hospital and offer to sell your blood. When I turned up, they turned me away – I turned out to be anaemic after a long summer's diet of beans on toast in London. It was a hungry train ride home.

The following spring, on a college trip to Kerry, one fine morning, climbing up the slopes of Mount Eagle, me with long hair and the patchy beginnings of a beard, dressed in hippie blouse and Indian beads, I passed an old farmer coming down the hill. 'Morning, Master Tuomey.' I ran after him, calling out, how could he know to greet me by my name? 'I recognise you out of your grandfather, your walk, you're the spit of him,' came the disarming reply. Impressed that anyone could manage to divine a resemblance between me and a dead man after nearly thirty-five years, him having drowned in 1938, me in my deep disguise and presuming myself free of family ties, I explained that I knew little of my grandfather and next to nothing of his history. He offered to arrange an introduction to the last living *seanchaí* on the Dingle peninsula, the very man who could tell me more. This storytelling character showed up later that day for tea and scones in the guesthouse kitchen, with the landlady listening in, him all the while holding on to my hand in a circular rocking motion. He let me in on local legends of my grandfather, wayward stories that had not been spoken of at home.

I began to imagine a scheme to reconnect with my seafaring grandfather, to plan the next summer's adventures working on the fishing boats out of Dingle. In a quayside pub I was introduced to a trawler captain, told him of my family connections with the sea, asked him for a start in June. He glared up unfriendly from his pint. 'Stick out your hands.' Taking my outstretched hands in his hard grip, he turned them over and back, showed them to the bar, roughly returned them to me. 'Post Office hands, you've never done a day's work in your life!' Outwardly humbled, but inwardly appreciative of escape from further humiliations, this chastening event marked the end of my short season in the manual labour market. I haven't strayed since from the drawing board.

I worked in and out of London, in and out of architecture, for three out of four summers during my college career. One summer I hitched up north from London to visit my girlfriend in Newcastle upon Tyne, staying longer than expected, working first on an archaeological dig in the city centre, then on a sociological survey. My girlfriend, on her year out from college, had made interesting feminist friends, a few of whom were involved with local council projects, and these contacts led to short-term contract work. For four weeks we dug down into a seventeenth-century pit at the Black Gate, finding only scraps of pottery, bits and pieces carefully dug out with trowels and cleaned up with toothbrushes. The archaeologists, discerning levels of history in changing colours of clay, took more interest in the layers of excavation than in any objects we found. Archaeology, I learned, is organised destruction. The polar opposite of the building site, which should be, at best, organised construction. Archaeology, you might say, is architecture in reverse. But, just like architects, archaeologists understand the world through things and places.

Then, for the next few weeks, briefed by social workers, my task was to seek out interviews along the lines of non-unionised men and women on the fish quays at North Shields. Working conditions were hard and inherently unequal, gutting and filleting fish in cold water sinks on the windy quayside, repetitive work for unreasonably varying rates of pay. Those who were dyeing fish for the smokehouses had permanently yellow-stained fingers.

We drank Madeira wine in one old pub, known locally for its nationally disproportionate consumption of countless barrels of this sticky stuff, a sawdust-floored dockers' pub with tilt-up cinema seats fixed along the walls.

We lived near the old Byker district, where the old grid-iron and hilly street system was being demolished and its residents rehoused in Scandinavian architect Ralph Erskine's sinuous so-called Byker Wall. Said to be designed to protect against traffic noise from the new ring road, it might also be seen as the built realisation of Erskine's earlier concept for an 'Arctic Town', with a high wrapping wall for shelter from icy snowstorms. The Byker was a distinctive district of stepped terraces, known as 'Tyneside flats', two-up two-down, two doors beside each other, one leading upstairs, the other into a ground-floor flat. Cast iron balcony stairs to narrow yards and lanes at the back. One woman showed us her bath hidden under a hinged wooden table-top. The living conditions were basic but the neighbourhood feeling was strong. The architect had his office in a corner shop and tried to work with community leaders to hold social structures in place despite the scale of slum clearance. A noble effort and an interesting experiment, dramatic to see its sweeping lines rising on the skyline. But it was hard to watch those red brick streets disappearing, week by week.

The summer before, with the same girlfriend, after a hard day's hitchhiking north from Arles, we got stranded on a dark roadside junction south of Lyon. Frustrated by the day's lack of progress, soaked in the pouring rain,

I stood out in the road and held up my hand to stop the next oncoming car. It was an old Rover. The driver acknowledged our misery and threw our wet rucksacks in the boot. We told him we were headed for Paris, had been hitching all day. After a few miles, he pulled into a commercial hotel and re-emerged to announce, 'Okay, we're off to Paris!' He'd cancelled his overnight booking. We tried to dissuade him, admitting we weren't in any real rush to get to Paris that night. 'Okay, let's take a detour,' he said. And thus began a magical episode that can only happen to the young and unready. He took us to a hidden village restaurant, treated us to all the local specialities, snails, frogs' legs, beef bourguignon, insisted we taste fine wines and cheeses, booked us in for the night and, over breakfast, proposed a scenic route through the vineyards of Burgundy and Champagne. We left him the next night, with six bottles of Vosne-Romanée added to our rucksacks. He checked us into a Paris hotel, refused to give his name or address, saying he wanted no thank you letters. In the course of our twenty-four-hour friendship, we learned that he was a survivor from the death camps of Dachau. He had vowed on his release to live for the moment, spontaneous at all times. A lesson in life's generosity.

Although most of my working life has been divided between London and Dublin, I suppose I could say I had a job in Africa, if only for six weeks. And this was immediately followed by a month in Milan. It was a miserable time, just one year after I got lucky in London and started working for James Stirling. Lonely nights lodging in a neutral hotel in Nairobi, then similarly stuck in Milan in the sweltering heat of August, when that city is seasonally abandoned by its inhabitants. Stirling was involved in a joint design project with Italian and African architects, a three-way creative collaboration the well-intentioned challenge set by the commissioning clients at the United Nations. That as yet unbuilt project was to be the African headquarters of the United Nations Environment Programme. The UN might have initially envisaged the Milan-based Giancarlo de Carlo as strategic master planner, with Stirling as flamboyant form-maker and Mutiso Menezes as executive architects local to Nairobi, a strategy that must have sounded credible in theory. In practice, all three architects preferred to think of themselves as fully involved in every aspect, with no agreed division of labour or territory between them. It was a painful process. My role was a sort of go-between, watchdog or guardian for Stirling's architectural concept, holding the fort in foreign service while the project passed through workshop sessions, travelling between three cities.

Each office had its own junior agent assigned to steer their ship through these rapids. Mostly, it was routine work, really just a change of location, similar drawing activities carried out in different places, but there were troubled days when sparks flew between participants, making it hot stuff for a young architect to handle. Once or twice I travelled to Geneva to hear Stirling present his concepts for the project to the UN clients. I was entrusted to stand by his design and, where necessary, fight his corner. 'No argy-bargy, if you can manage it,' was his brief to me. And, of course, as might be expected, there were occasional, sometimes exotic, days out to break the tedium of covert spying and overt peacekeeping, enough to allow for some honest fun between the parties.

Nairobi was a volatile place for a working visitor. You were neither a sight-seeing safari-suited tourist like other guests in the hotel, nor an independent traveller, more a random observer of the world outside the window. The wide avenues were filled with life, men getting shaved under trees, barbers' broken mirrors nailed to the trees, people milling about at bus stops, tall Maasai stalking into town with heads held high. There could be spontaneous outbursts of violence, bag-snatchers chased down the boulevards, getting tangled up in barbed wire man-traps camouflaged under the pretty banks of bougainvillea planted along the central road reservations. And then you had to hear them, perpetrator turned victim, being beaten up by the baying crowd. Queueing for the cinema was strangely discomfiting, with cruelly crippled beggars pushing their hands into your pockets, a feeling of fear everywhere on the streets; white immigrants, then categorised as expats, directed up onto the balcony level, an altogether agitating experience, nothing like the urbane anonymity of London picture-going. And the movies themselves usually terrible. The mostly white technical and professional classes stuck close together and socialised in the suburbs, hosting barbecues on their wide-verandaed bungalows, visiting airline crews among the star attractions, and, on the margins of those five-acre properties, shed-like outhouses for the houseboys to sleep in. Divisive conditions that made me feel awkward, a social disengagement unspoken but tacitly accepted across the section of society I met at work.

We were taken on a big safari, carried in convoys of jeeps out into the national park, flying in a single-propeller plane around the slopes of Kilimanjaro and along pink-fringed lakes, the poor flamingos disturbed into flight, buzzing low over frightened herds of giraffe and wildebeest. We were brought back to an evening feast, watching elephants washing themselves by convenient waterholes – who knows how they were led to congregate at these tourist traps. We were entertained by astonishing high-jump performances from Maasai men in traditional dress. Exploitation of man and beast. The wrong introduction to Africa. The entire episode, vulgar displays and displaced values, not for me.

Despite the muggy heat of summer, Milan came as a relief to the mind. The air in Nairobi was fresh and clear, but the social atmosphere was stifling. Now I was in Italy, closer to where I belonged. I lived in another anonymous hotel, mostly empty, it being August. The cinema was nearby. I saw Derek Jarman's *Sebastiane*, dialogue spoken in Latin and dubbed into Italian, appropriately enough. I could walk the short distance to work. My colleagues at de Carlo's office were friendly, de Carlo himself avuncular and amenable to conversation with a young apprentice. He worked overhead in a small room accessed by a red spiral stair. He gave me his old Bakelite Swiss-made rotary pencil sharpener, admiring how much I admired it. I still use it at my drawing desk every day. His project architect, a sympathetic Swiss woman, had a tiny flat that opened onto a huge pergola-covered roof terrace, and an outdoor kitchen where I learned to cook saltimbocca *alla romana*.

We drove to Verona to see *Aida*. Twenty thousand people gathered outdoors in a Roman arena, evidence of a culture where grand opera is a popular event. Just as the audience worked themselves up to the thrill of the triumphal march, the stagehands staged a lightning strike, right at the start of the second act, declaring that the show would not go on unless their terms were met. The crowd instantly divided into those who felt solidarity for the strikers and those who felt unfairly denied the glory of the music they had come to hear. Angry exchanges ignited between people who had been peaceably seated beside one another. Programmes were waved in the air, old folks in overcoats cheering and shouting like hooligans at a football match. Then another announcement, a good twenty minutes into the strike. The workers' claims had been settled. Everybody sat down, the orchestra played and on came the parade. And then the singing. People were weeping and whispering, 'Bellissima!' It was magnificent. Like a scene from Fellini played out in real life. The real Italy. Unforgettable. Then back to the real life in London.

Learning from Stirling

I believe that the shapes of a building should indicate –
perhaps display – the usage and way of life of its
occupants, and it is therefore likely to be rich and varied
in appearance, and its expression is unlikely to be simple.
James Stirling, 'An Architect's Approach to Architecture'

I JOINED JAMES STIRLING's office in September 1976,
working late hours through the length of four years until
my return to Dublin. Straight out of college, working
for my hero, my first proper job, the critical years in my
formation as an architect. My thesis project had been
a Constructivist-inspired newspaper office aligned on
the axis of Dublin's O'Connell Street. Encouraged by
a sympathetic tutor, I posted nine postcard-size black-
and-white drawings, together with a handwritten
letter expressing my enthusiasm for the work. I spoke
briefly to Stirling on the phone one Friday evening – a
very short interview – 'Nice drawings, actually. When
can you start?' – and turned up for work the next
Monday morning.

I was despatched to the basement, where I spent most
of the days and nights of the following four years. The
mornings began quietly with classical music on Radio 3; by
mid-afternoon the air was thick with cigar smoke. Evenings
were loud with the Rolling Stones and Bob Marley on a

reel-to-reel tape recorder. 'I know it's only rock and roll but I like it.' 'Lively up yourself.' Conversations included the possibility of reincarnation in the form of your chosen classical composer; one bagged Beethoven, another opted for Brahms, I was assigned to Schubert. Lists were a daily pastime in those team-working days; name your top ten Le Corbusier buildings, top ten buildings of all time, top ten Dylan songs, and on it went.

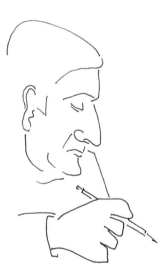

Stirling dropped down from time to time throughout the day, sometimes bringing wine and cigars after his dinner at home, keeping a careful eye on every detail, keeping competition designs moving in the direction he wanted things to go. On one such occasion, late in the evening, when we were working on the competition draw-up for the Neue Staatsgalerie Stuttgart, he appeared from upstairs.

We were engaged in one of those regular downstairs chats. I suppose we must have been making too much chatter while, at his end of the table, he was trying to concentrate. We had worked our way through questions of invention and quotation. We were just moving on to our top ten Frank Lloyd Wright buildings of all time when Stirling called a halt. He held up his page of intensely active drawings. He had noted down each topic of our discussion, adding his own closing instruction, pleading for peace and quiet, which he read out slowly and in a loud voice – 'End of conversation!' When I look today at that much-published sketch, it brings me back to the close confinement and camaraderie of those basement days.

At that time, over the preceding seven years, Stirling had not had a single new commission leading to a built building. No wonder people found him a little melancholy and sometimes brusque. Yet, despite this lack of client confidence and without any commercial success, he remained critically regarded, not just by friends in London and followers in Dublin, but in every corner of the connected culture, as the greatest architect in the world.

The breakthrough burst of early work, four closely consecutive and individually brilliant university buildings, from Leicester through to St Andrews and on to Cambridge and Oxford, had been completed in just eight years between 1963 and 1971. He had been a visiting professor at Yale since 1968. The so-called 'black book', published in Germany in 1974, charted the flow of his creativity across those lost years, almost a decade of ground-breaking work that never made it to construction. And then, following that elegant publication, came a sequence of German competitions, two unplaced designs for new museums in Düsseldorf and Cologne, and, at last, in 1977, the career reviving competition winning scheme for the Neue Staatsgalerie Stuttgart. It had been a slow climb back to building and times had been tough. The office effectively started again after the Stuttgart win.

I wasn't much involved in the development of the early stages of the Stuttgart competition entry, helping out in only a minor way during the final draw-up. The project concept had been developed from one short and simple instruction issued before Stirling disappeared on summer holiday – 'Make it a Düsseldorf mark 2.' So, by this diktat, before the emergence of any new thoughts specific to the project in hand, there was going to have to be a circular courtyard, a mid-block pedestrian path, a curved glazed lobby and a top-lit gallery sequence.

A few of us had been laid off after the competition submission deadline, since there was no more work for us to do in London. As it happened, Sheila (my girlfriend then, now my wife and partner) was laid off that very same day, work having dried up at her job too. So we set off for Rome with friends from the office, four of us piled into a VW beetle. This trip, travelling down through Switzerland, introduced us to new work in Ticino. We visited long and tall concrete houses on sloping sites. We stopped at Bissone, the birthplace of Borromini. We discovered Terragni in Como, spaghetti alle vongole in

Rome, as well as the Pantheon and the whole panoply of the Roman baroque.

One day, coming back into Rome after an outing to Hadrian's Villa, worrying about things back in London, we went into the post office to call the office. Stirling was cross. 'Where the hell are you? We've won Stuttgart, what are you doing in Rome?' He was reminded that we'd been fired. 'Well, get back here immediately!' We came back straightaway, me to return to my desk in the basement and Sheila to start her master's at the Royal College of Art. I had been shortlisted to take up a scholarship at the British School at Rome, with the genial Bob Maxwell as my tutor, but that was the end of that.

As soon as the office was reassembled, the Stuttgart clients had to be reassured by a studio visit. They needed to know that the London office was capable of carrying out such a large building. On the day of their visit, friends and colleagues were borrowed to fill up empty desks and told to look busy. Stirling led a tour of the basement. He stopped at my desk to introduce me to the gallery directors, saying, 'John's one of our senior architects. How long is it you are with us now, John? Seven or eight years it must be?', and quickly moving on before they could question the youth or uncover the inexperience of this long-haired recently graduated non-German-speaking student type.

The culture changed from free-ranging short-span competition deadlines to one of slow steady work, a painstaking production of working drawings and learning from first principles about German building regulations.

It was a long jump from the established language of Stirling's architecture to the technical demands of European construction. German regulations required all railings to have a maximum spacing of 100mm, sufficient to prevent the passage of a baby's head through any gap in the upstand. Ship's railings were the Stirling office standard, thin tubular steel bars, wide-spaced and horizontal in emphasis, like those on the deck of a liner. Stirling was not ready to change his mind on matters like this. After a lot of soul-searching by the project team, the problem was solved by Stirling himself. Not diverging from the two-bar principle, we were told simply to increase the diameter of the tubes until all regulatory requirements could be met. This was described as a transition from 'thin-man railings' to 'fat-man railings'. No compromise at all. Although, it has to be said, real ship's railings were mostly white, sometimes black or grey, never pink and blue.

Above my desk in the basement bow window, one floor below Stirling's desk upstairs, hung the framed original of the famous little worm's-eye view of the Oxford Queen's College student residence known as the Florey Building, a particularly fine-line ink drawing, and a particular favourite of mine. After-drawings were made partly for publication purposes, partly to 'fix' the design. They were made in the aftermath, part of the routine in the wind-down days following a competition entry or during the post-completion period of a building, made to capture some crucial aspects of the form, to illustrate the conceptual structure.

Presentation drawings were set up precisely, first in accurately drawn pencil underlay and then traced over using a studied selection of 0.18 and 0.13 Rotring Isograph pens. The thicker line weight of a 0.25 nib might be sometimes sparingly allowed, for instance to emphasise a section line, but this was best avoided. This was a demanding skill, requiring grease-free page preparation and a steady hand. Inked lines had to join exactly at the corners, closing cleanly with no crossover or variation in thickness. The pen had to be held vertically. You must never let the nib lean into the bevelled edge of your adjustable setsquare. Curved lines, whether drawn along French curves or set out with a compass, had to seamlessly connect with straight lines, with no trace of the point of transition. When mistakes were made, as they must be from time to time, the ink-line had to be scratched off the surface of the page with a razor blade, then the surface made perfectly smooth by rubbing with an eraser or polished with the back of your fingernail, then the new line added back exactly in its place with no visible evidence of repair work. This was a question of honour among the aficionados of the art. It was important to keep the drawing clean and dry, no sweaty hands, including protecting against the risk of damage from the large and sweaty hands of the big man himself.

I had arrived in the office assuming I knew how to draw. After all, I had studiously modelled my student drawings on Stirling's drawing style. I knew the sources. I knew the regulating lines of early Le Corbusier elevations. I was steeped in the graphic culture of Russian Constructivism. I thought I knew what I was doing. But I soon found I could not compete with the intimidating speed of the real experts in the field of Rotring ink work. In these elevated circles, I simply wasn't fast enough. I could crawl with confidence, but I couldn't run.

At least my UCD training had equipped me with the necessary skills in pencil draughtsmanship. We'd had a number of American-educated tutors at UCD, men who had shown us how to draw in pencil. From them we learned the tricks of the trade, how to rotate the pencil as you draw to keep a sharp and unvarying line, how to work your way down the page, always moving from right to left, to keep the drawing from getting dirty, when to change the lead in your clutch pencil from F to H to allow for changes in humidity as the day wore on into evening. This training proved an effective and useful preparation for the Stirling office culture.

One part of my work on Stuttgart became the resolution of the steel and glass canopies, a family of industrial-style elements, overhanging each of the public entry points to the building like railway station structures. Stirling was out of town and I had to make a start. I began drawing the canopies from underneath. Looking from this point of view clarified the inner shape of the structures, a shape that couldn't be properly described in plan or section. I suppose I thought I was working in the office tradition, something like the well-known worm's-eye drawings I looked at every day. I can see now that I was held back by my lack of technical knowledge from any attempt at fixing details. The drawings were simply large-scale design studies. Three of these drawings were well under way and all spread out on my desk, representing several days' concentrated work, when Stirling suddenly appeared in the office, back from wherever he had been, maybe teaching at Yale. He was in a testy and impatient mood. Why was I spending time on these big drawings? They didn't look much like working drawings. We needed to be working effectively to get the bloody working drawings done and ready for German approval. I thought I'd better keep low and stay out of trouble.

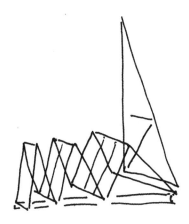

He took one of the drawings away with him. Later that day he called me on the phone and asked me to come upstairs. 'Nice drawings actually, how many have we got?' Three, I replied. 'Do you think you could make three more? You see, I think MoMA want a set of six, actually.' I looked over his shoulder, at his own drawing desk. He had begun what would turn out to be a tediously slow sky-colouring process, using blue and purple Derwent pencils in a graded sort of cross-hatching. This was a new departure. Interesting. And I was out of trouble. I don't remember how long Stirling spent colouring them in. He sat upstairs at his desk for days, listening to Radio 3, happy in his work. When the work was done, with six drawings finished and all coloured up, he called me upstairs again. This time with an amiable question.

'How would you describe these drawings?'

'Well, I suppose they could be described as worm's-eye planar axonometrics.'

'Hmm ... I was thinking of up-view full frontals, what do you think?'

Colour was important to Stirling, not in the usual tasteful way, neither soft nor sensitive, more a flash of contrariness, like a sign of life, or a spice of life. He wore purple socks that livened up the ankle-space between his grey flannel trousers and his sand-coloured desert boots. Every day. He wore blue cotton shirts and spotted knitted ties. Every day the same. Relentless. Once when he went on his usual family summer holiday to Normandy, he asked Sheila and me to move in to Belsize Park to look after the house while they were away. His wardrobe was neatly shelved in stacks of identical shirts. Drawers full of purple socks. Spotted ties hung in rows. No surprises there.

At the end of one of his public lectures, someone asked a question. Not the usual question – why had he changed his style, was he now a post-modernist, what were we to make of this new work? This person wanted to know whether, given how many different projects he had designed over so many years, he agreed that careful analysis would reveal that he'd had only five ideas across his lengthy career. He wasn't much taken aback, as I recall. He thought for a moment before he replied, 'Only five ideas. Well, I suppose that's three more than Mies – and five more than Gropius!'

In July 1984, three years after our return to Dublin, we interrupted, no, extended, our honeymoon in Venice, taking the train to Stuttgart to join an office party to celebrate the opening of the Neue Staatsgalerie. Charles Jencks, a well-known architecture critic, was there to see the building. We joined them for lunch in the gallery café. Jencks was teasing Stirling that the building looked unfinished. The drum lacked a dome. The architect was teasing the critic about the cumbersome lens on his camera. Male jewellery. Later on, we walked around while Jencks took his photos. A passing stranger stopped us on the stepped ramp, recognising the stout figure of the architect from pictures in the local newspaper. He shook hands with Stirling, saying in broken English how beautiful the building was. Jim was more than pleased. Shy. Proud. He turned to me and said, 'There must be something wrong with it, John, everybody seems to like it!'

Let Us Go Then

Let us go then, you and I
When the evening is spread out against the sky
       T.S. Eliot, 'The Love Song of J. Alfred Prufrock'

I FIRST MET SHEILA, my life's companion, in the first week of
our first-year studies at UCD. She had long straight hair,
parted in a dead straight line down the centre. Something
refined about her quiet presence. I noticed her the first
day in the studio. We had our first significant conversation
when we bumped into each other, each a little lost, on the
landing at the Saturday night student dance. We talked
for a good half hour, or maybe more, standing halfway
down the central stair in the nested-tables composition
of the concrete-frame Restaurant Building that was then,
still is, the best building on the Belfield campus. This
was a noisy, crowded place for any kind of meeting of
minds, but we managed to cover quite a bit of territory
in our introductory exchange. We spoke about feelings of
relief that school life was behind us, and our excitement
about the new life in college ahead of us. We shared our
enthusiasm for the language of Eliot's 'Prufrock'; the poem
had been so different in kind and structure from anything
else on our school curriculum, the long poem that leads
to an overwhelming question not being asked. Both of

us knew nearly every line of that poem, as it turned out. Common ground discovered. This was the beginning of my grown-up life.

Sheila is smart. Highly analytical. A little shy, sometimes hesitant. Green-eyed. Far-seeing. Forensic. Fond of maps. Meticulous. Reflective. We established an instant empathy, a firm friendship ensued, an undeclared courtship that took five years to come to the point of forming a couple. I always say I knew, from that very first day, that we were meant to be together. Of course, even if I'd only guessed then at the possibility, one of a number of possibilities, given that we each sustained other serious relationships throughout our student years, I can say now I was on the right track from the start.

We set out together at the end of our final term at UCD, inspired by days in the library poring over drawings of Italian gardens of the Renaissance, seeking first-hand experience of what we'd been reading, wanting to explore architecture, to begin again, to find our own way. We felt that our student work had been misunderstood, unfairly disregarded. We needed to get away. Disgruntled, we did not come back for the graduation ceremony in September, which must have been a disappointment to Sheila's father, university professor and Dean of the Faculty of Engineering and Architecture, who was master of ceremonies at that event. He might have been looking forward to the formal handshake with his brilliant daughter. Still, he didn't hold it against us, not in the long run.

We had drawn up our thesis projects in Sheila's parents' house, taking over the family dining room while they were away on a foreign trip. They returned late one night to find the house filled with drawing boards, rolls of paper, and four exhausted students in the last run-up to their final presentations. It must have been a surprise, but they didn't flinch, never complained about our late-night wailing along with Joni Mitchell's *Court and Spark*. We worked late and started late. Early each morning Sheila and I would stroll under the apple trees in the garden to see the dawn, I'd go to my flat to sleep, and we would start again the next day with lunch for breakfast eaten in their kitchen. One year later, her parents came to visit us in London, a tacit recognition of their acceptance of our living in sin. We decided to treat them as equals, condescending to bring them to eat and drink in our regular haunts. We chose cheap Chinese restaurants to see if they could cope with the cuisine, only to hear of their recent experiences in rural night markets in China. We were a little worried they might not fit in to the Soho clatter of the French House, but we dared walk them in without any advance preparation. 'Ah, and do they still have that little café upstairs?' asked her father. Upstaged by Sheila's ever-sophisticated parents. Later in those London years, we came back to visit them on their Easter holidays in Kerry. Sheila's mother had made a delicious tea cake, cut in thick buttered slices, the plate handed around the table one more time for second helpings. 'It won't pass Tuomey!' was the Prof's way of making me feel at home.

After that post-student summer's wanderings, Paris for me, searching out lost shadows of Le Corbusier, Utrecht for Sheila, following the trail of Dutch social housing from the 1930s, it didn't take us long to get ourselves redirected, reunited and settled into life in London. We lodged for a while in the Brixton home of an architectural historian who had kindly adopted us as friends, one of the UCD 'flying circus' of visiting lecturers who had encouraged us as students to study further outside the narrow curriculum. I'd spent part of a previous summer in London living in his house as a lodger, babysitting his son and daughter, learning how to cook like a family man, learning about Cuban architecture after the revolution, picking up the basics of the Chinese game of Go. When I turned up again, two years later, hungry and tired off the ferry from France, his daughter greeted me cheerily in her south London accent, "Allo John, we 'aven't seen you in long days!"

Once we got working, we moved from the warmth of this lovely lefty-liberal house into a lightless basement in Tufnell Park and then on to another in Bloomsbury, before landing on our feet in a high-ceilinged rent-free flat in Primrose Hill. The landlord was prepared to grant us a temporary licence to occupy the vacant ground floor of an otherwise long-term tenanted house on a quiet square. It suited his purposes to protect his property from squatters while avoiding any further tenant's entitlements. All we had to do was a little basic plumbing, simple rewiring and surface refurbishment. We painted the walls white and the floorboards blue. We loved the spatial luxury of these elegant and empty rooms, draughty and cold in winter, airy in summer, perfect light for drawing up projects and plenty of space for cycling around indoors during post-deadline parties, speeches made standing on the wide stone mantelpiece, a stone's throw from Chalk Farm Tube station, my first portal into life in London.

Having moved out of Brixton and subsumed ourselves into the world of work, we lost touch with our old tutor, whose generous hospitality we might be said to have taken for granted. Lost touch for many years, until he wrote out of the blue to wish us well, having read of a recent architectural award in *The Observer*. We'd been shortlisted for the Stirling Prize, a prize that has eluded us despite a teasing number of near misses. I'd been living with him when I first got my job with Stirling. In the meantime, we, all three of us, had moved on from London. We were delighted to hear from him, eager to return his hospitality, immediately invited him to come to visit us in Connemara. How would we get on after thirty-five years? Would we even recognise each other when we met? And now he was due to arrive in three weeks. We were returning from a London site visit, stopping on the way to Heathrow for tea at the London Review Cake Shop. Sitting on the bench seat in that tiny café, we noticed something familiar in the voice, the Castro beard, the rotational hand gestures of the somewhat elderly individual settling down beside us as he ordered his tea. Yes, it was him, the very same man, utterly unchanged except in years. Out of the whole crowded metropolis, the millions coming and going in and out of London that day, we'd found each other without looking, sitting side by side in a literary café, reunited by a chance encounter, and fell to talking as if time was no distance at all. 'We haven't seen you in long days.' When, soon after, he came to stay in Connemara, we walked the long beaches like old friends, comparing ways to keep close to our fast-growing-up children, sharing memory-jolting methods for enhanced communication with fathers slowly dying.

Among the architects working in Stirling's basement there were a few racing-bike enthusiasts, leg-shavers as they were known. Their energy was infectious. Soon I was spending Saturday mornings at a bicycle-building shop on Portobello Road, debating the merits of Reynolds double-butted tubing, all-Shimano brake parts, Brooks saddles and fifteen-shift derailleurs. They had the bones of my custom-made bike up on the work bench for those few weeks. Lean-sinewed old guys would gather round to offer advice. 'With your elbow propped against the prow of the saddle, you should just be able to flip the handlebars with your fingertips.' Or, on another day, 'Always remember, you cycle in circles!' Bad advice this, apparently; it's now considered better for pedalling power to cycle in half-circles, pushing down then pulling back. In the main, we cycled short distances commuting around the city, wasting the potential of our lightweight and elegant machines. But we toured further afield for holidays; Palladio villas of the Veneto, the bastide towns of the Dordogne, Santiago de Compostela and the granite landscapes of Galicia. The freedom of cycling – one minute you're crying uphill against the wind, the next coasting downhill under clear skies, fifty feelings felt intensely in a single day. The bible of *Richard's Bicycle Book*, which included practical advice on dealing with *chiens méchants* – it's the sound of the spinning spokes that drives them mad – stand your ground and keep the bike between you and the dog. Apart from this, for the freewheeling life, all you need is a foldable map, a compact puncture repair kit tucked under your saddle, plus a few changes of clothes in your two pannier bags.

One night, after a long day's cycling in the Dordogne, we stopped at the Hotel de la Paix in Monpazier, right in the middle of the medieval grid-town. Its arcaded market square of individuated houses, known to us from Le Corbusier's travel writings, was built in freestanding plots so that each house could be allowed to burn down separately if ever the town came under siege. The *patron* and his sole guest, an old Belgian train driver, were friends from their youth, having competed against each other in the Tour de France. We were welcomed as fellow cyclists, though we were nowhere near the competitive level of our new-found companions. First the *patron* took care of the bicycles, hanging them up in the barn to relieve undue pressure on the tyres. Then the engine-driver persuaded the hotelier of his own perfectly logical understanding of the principle of the *menu-prix-fixe*. If everybody in the restaurant eats the same fare, with no variations, so much the more economical for the kitchen. And so all three of us, the only guests in the hotel, shared an extended feast of cordon bleu cooking for the price of a simple plat du jour. La charcuterie maison, paté de foie gras, truites aux amandes, tarte tatin. I recall every dish, a banquet out of our league at the time. The brotherhood of the bicycle opened doors that otherwise would have stayed shut.

We cycled into the granite city of Santiago de Compostela on St James's Day, to find it was a Holy Year, and the Cathedral's Holy Door would be open, a once in eleven-year event. The Holy Door being open, the giant incense thurible could be swung properly from its pulleys, ropes pulled by eight men running from side to side, the barrel-sized censer sweeping across the altar and the lateral naves, smoke billowing as it flew through space, a most impressive sight. Galicia was almost empty of tourists. This was before the revival in popularity of the Camino. We ate caldo gallego every night, a bacon, cabbage and white bean stew. One night we struggled through what must have been a bucketload of percebes – goose barnacles – like lizard legs, long, black and horridly chewy. 'A dish fit for a cardinal,' we were told. Hard to swallow nonetheless. We relished the taste of firm white steaks of merluza, which, it was explained to us, was hake freshly caught in Irish waters. We cycled to Spain to discover our own native fish. On the country roads, we rode past solid-wooden-wheeled carts pulled by pairs of oxen. In the fields, we saw long narrow stone-slatted corn stores, raised up on granite piers. The seaside village of Combarro, with big lumps of rock rising right out of the road, felt like an open air set for a real life Synge play. The whole stony landscape was a step back in time. And yet, this weirdly different place, remote and distant as it was, seemed strangely familiar when looked at through Irish eyes.

We were Irish in London through the 1970s and early '80s, but considered ourselves outside the cultural category of the London Irish, far removed from the loneliness and loss of the mailboat-displaced emigrant generation of the 1950s and '60s. We thought of ourselves as belonging to a new crop of European Irish, cosmopolitans of a cross-national, anti-nationalist inclination. Our London employers, of course, saw us as Irish, liked us for this, maybe envied our sense of identity, made us feel welcome wherever we went. The London we admired was a reflection of Britain's post-war, civic-spirited, reconstructed society. Its National Health Service, its social housing programme. We enjoyed its down-at-heel liberalism and benefited from its tradition of measured tolerance. All of this civility has unravelled long since, but not then, not until the rot set in when Mrs Thatcher allowed herself to declare, 'There is no such thing as society.'

We liked to think of ourselves in some sort of devotional continuity with the architecture culture of our tutors and mentors, drinking at the York Minster, the so-called French House, where the Brutalists of the 1950s

used to meet on Saturday mornings. No sign of them
when we showed up, but still a wonderful place for fevered
discussion between sips of Pernod and downing bottles of
wine. It became our spiritual home for the time being. We
spent nights staring at the black-and-white photographs
framed in a frieze along its walls. Dreaming up life
adventures for the long-distance cyclist Lilian Dredge,
with her racing bicycle at full tilt on her lonely way from
Land's End to John O'Groats. Talking with regulars like
Chicago the boxer, the 'Chicago Kid', who had once boxed
in Kilkenny. He held his own at the corner of the bar,
answering every question with affable resignation – 'Could
be better and could be worse, but by the grace of God, I live
to fight another day.' Talking with Ron the boiler-coverer,
who taxied in every Thursday evening from his home in
the East End. We met the man who drew Biffo the Bear
for the *Beano*, a pinstripe-suited gent with a rose in his
lapel. Gaston Berlemont, the *patron*, who told us he had
been born in the bar, became another avuncular figure in
our London life.

Sometimes, half-ashamed of ourselves, half-lonely for
home, we slipped down, dipped down, into the basement
pub built into the Underground at Piccadilly Circus.
Ward's Irish House was well established as a landmark
before the self-styled Irish pub became an international
brand-marketing phenomenon, penetrating cities well
beyond the diaspora. Ward's was divided into rooms
around a central zinc-topped bar, rooms named for the four
provinces, Munster and Leinster, Ulster and Connacht.

One night, having settled ourselves in the Leinster lounge, maybe one foot in Munster, no feeling of entitlement to the other two, Sheila made her way up to the bar to order another couple of pints. She was approached by a besuited man on the make, on for a chat, keen to try his luck – would she pull up a stool? She pointed to the long-haired bespectacled fellow over there in the corner, explained why she was at the bar, it being her turn to buy the drinks. He eyed me up with a single glance, turned back to her, his back to me, to repeat his offer, adding, I'm told, by way of persuasion, 'You'll never get anywhere with that hypothetical-looking fucker!'

London's rudest restaurant was well hidden down the tiny passage of Rupert Court. The lane-facing room looked small and inviting, an authentic hideaway in Chinatown, big pots of steaming noodles and flattened ducks hanging in the window, Chinese people at every table. Might we find a vacant seat in some cosy corner? We never found out. 'Upstair please!' came the cry from all sides, and upstairs we went every time. The best available table in this vertically stacked, racially stratified restaurant was by the first-floor window overlooking the neon-lit laneway, within touching distance, almost, of the building opposite, like a big ship docked in a busy harbour. Simple fare, very tasty, swiftly served, no complaints. Once, with visiting family to impress, we asked for dishes to be served in sequence, starting with Peking duck and pancakes for all to share. 'This no high-class restaurant! Food ready, you eat!' Ah, we loved the old Wong Kei. 'Upstair please!'

And sometimes, to clear the palate after Chinese food, we made our way through Soho to Bernigra's for an ice cream cone, noce or sorbetto al limone, or an espresso lungo at the Bar Italia, and then back to the French House for a nightcap glass of port. We had emerged from a monoculture where everybody's ethnicity was the same. Holy Catholic Ireland, not ever wholly Catholic, but altogether homogenous nonetheless. Now we were relishing the change to multicultural London, out and about in the downtown metropolis, its distinctive differences maintained in close adjacency, so handily side by side for us to mix and match. All the while discussing, over noodles, ice cream, coffee and our next choice of alcohol, the meaning or the message of some new European film seen earlier in the evening.

More about ice cream. The ice cream shop local to Primrose Hill, Marine Ices at Chalk Farm, had franchises in cinemas and theatres around London, halfway downstairs to the Gate in the Brunswick Centre, on the way into the Screens on the Green and the Hill, and, most memorably, in the foyer at the Royal Court. We went with a friend to see, to watch, to witness Billie Whitelaw in Beckett's *Happy Days*. Three seats right in the middle of the very front row, spitting distance from the centre of the action on stage, or lack of action, given the restricted action of this great play. Marine Ices were on sale at the interval. The theatre was hot, the performance intense, why not three pistachio cones to cool us down? Sooner than expected, the bell called the audience back to their seats ... 'between the bell for waking and the bell for sleeping'. And there she was, the magnificent Winnie, uncomplaining, up to her neck in a mound of scorched earth, under the heat of the stage lights. And there we were, well within her spitting distance, closer than the first act by some stage magic, licking our ice creams. One by one, quickly and quietly, we slipped those subversive cones under our seats, ashamed by the contrast between our stupid behaviour and her stoic example. Live theatre is never the same as cinema. Another lesson learned.

London was an extended education for us, a second schooling in how to live like architects, with the regular stimulus of lectures and exhibitions at the Architectural Association on Bedford Square or Peter Cook's rallies at Art Net, just around the corner from the AA. We learned to cook from Elizabeth David's *Italian Food*, this old classic first, then moving on to her *French Provincial Cooking*. Both paperbacks survive, battered and burnt, in our kitchen today. If you can read you can soon cook, and the more attentive the reading, the better the cooking. We went to the cinema as often as we could manage, to the Phoenix East Finchley, the Gate in Notting Hill or down in the basement of the Brunswick Centre, or to the Academy in Oxford Street where they made their own hand-printed posters for every film screened. It was a time when European cinema could be looked to for moral enlightenment, film directors being the poets and philosophers of our generation. Late-night movies were part of our daily routine. Wim Wenders's cinema-loving *Kings of the Road*. Werner Herzog's mysterious *Enigma of Kasper Hauser.* The playful fantasy of Jacques Rivette's *Céline and Julie Go Boating.* The longitudinal loggias of the Lombardy barns that formed the backdrop to Ermanno Olmi's *Tree of the Wooden Clogs.* Agnès Varda's brightly feminist *One Sings, the Other Doesn't.* Sam Peckinpah's sad-eyed and lonely *Pat Garret and Billy the Kid*, with Bob Dylan in a cameo role as Alias – 'Alias who? Alias Alias.'

We came out of the cinema one Saturday night to find people lining the streets in Soho, waiting for Bob Dylan concert tickets to go on sale at Cambridge Circus on the Sunday morning. I trotted home to pick up sleeping bags while Sheila took her place in the queue. The streets filled up quickly. We spent the night stretched out on the wide footpath of Old Compton Street, not so much sleeping as singing along with everyone else. Dylan's songs, badly sung, filled the night. Then, in the fourth row at the Earl's Court concert, the *Street Legal* concert, the people sitting around us were the ones we had sung with in the street, tickets having been sold in strict order and limited to four per person. It was a feeling of fellowship, a community of the faithful, the first and greatest of the several Dylan concerts we have seen. Our seats were so close to the stage, we felt he was singing just for us. The following month, we joined the hordes to watch him again on the airfield in Blackbushe, a different audience of more than 200,000 people. The troubadour himself wore a different disguise, white-face under a black top hat. We arrived back in Waterloo station in the early hours of the morning, all dazed as if waking out of a dream. 'Don't look back.'

'Will you ever go back?' was the late-night question asked of every Irish-in-London by every other passing émigré. The perennial question. Then, when you do get around to returning home, you're likely to be asked in the street, 'Are you back, or what?' It's difficult to stay away. And it's difficult to settle back in. In our case, despite the privilege of creative places for work and study, me at Stirling's studio, Sheila at the RCA, we had begun to feel the slow tug homeward. We found ourselves coming around to the realisation that going back was turning into a mutual plan. 'Let us go then, you and I.' Dublin would be the next step in this work–life adventure, with the bedrock of marriage, the wonder of children, forty years' absorption in architectural education and the trial by fire of studio practice to fill our days.

Looking Back

Wordsworth? ... No. I'm afraid we're not familiar with
your literature, Lieutenant. We feel closer to the warm
Mediterranean. We tend to overlook your little island.
                              Brian Friel, *Translations*

SO WE DID GO back, back home to Dublin, to begin again.

I arrived first, living in a tiny bedsit on the half-
landing of a house on Elgin Road, half-living in London
still. Sheila followed a year or so later and we moved up in
the world, albeit to another basement flat, just around the
corner in Wellington Road. A German friend had sent us
on our way out of London, using faux-football parlance
to tease us non-football fans, with strict instructions to
'change the face of Irish architecture!' We had a hunch
to step away from the London scene, antagonistic as we
were to post-modern distractions on the rise. We wouldn't
thrive unless we got out. After four years of late nights and
long weekends in the basement of 75 Gloucester Place,
sometimes working on three different sketch designs a
day, I wanted more than churning out options for James
Stirling to adopt or deny.

I joined the Office of Public Works in the autumn of
1980. I worked in New Works V at 7 Ely Place, thinking
of myself like a doctor in a public hospital, or a teacher
in a school. You do the work you're asked to do, the work

that needs to be done. Away from the commercial world, no competitive pressure, no touting for work, the file lands on your desk with neutral instructions, asking you to report how best to proceed with the job. This was the idea, making a useful contribution to public work. Life in the civil service was not so simple as it sounds. It was slow moving. Things were hard to speed up. I missed the studio culture, the project-driven engine room of private practice. I was first assigned to design a new headquarters for the Public Record Office, an ambitiously large building that was soon stopped due to lack of funds, probably a lucky escape for me and for the city. I had expected to work on typical buildings, pattern buildings like the national school I'd attended in Cooley, designed as prototypes, never exactly the same in plan but composed from similar elements. Or minor civic structures like the post offices built on the streets of provincial towns. Those days were gone. I managed to get two buildings built in my seven years at the OPW, both atypical, specialist one-off buildings, a laboratory and a courthouse, more suitably modest in scale, more convincing in their cross-sectional arrangement of parts than in their external expression, I can see that now, but a credible step towards competency nonetheless.

The job allowed for dedicated involvement from inception to completion; from briefing, analysis, design and working drawings through to construction and contract management. I'd never set foot in a real site meeting before I had to run my first one. I'm grateful for the opportunity offered to an inexperienced young architect. Such a combination of responsibility and relative autonomy would be hard to find nowadays and remains deserving of respect. On the day I left the OPW, the boss of my section took me out for a pint, with solemn words imparted to one setting out in private practice – 'Never refuse conversation with a seemingly solvent stranger.' Very different from James Stirling's admonishment when asked how to approach my return to Dublin after years abroad – 'With fists flying!' Neither piece of advice was acted upon, or proved itself useful in practice, not that I can recall.

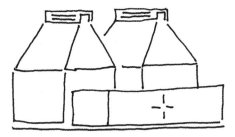

I drove out one day to show a visiting French architect my very first building, a meat-testing laboratory in Abbottstown, still the State Farm at that time. This was before that building had been carefully renovated, restored as if it were a protected structure, but then, alas, much less sympathetically extended. That fine day, before any of those changes were made, we picked up a white-coated scientist as he walked along the driveway, whistling his way back from lunch. We asked for directions, the road layout having changed. I described the twin-roofed volume of the building – 'Ah, you mean Picasso's Tits!' He told us what he thought of this 'modernist collage', unaware that the architect was with him in the car. I like this habit of nicknaming buildings. Another project, the Irish Pavilion, was christened the Mouse-Museum by its Dutch curators. A neighbouring resident, also unawares, stopping to chat while I looked over the wall at a nearly completed house, described the complex roof formation of our design as 'two cockroaches unsuccessfully mating'. And more recently, our Seán O'Casey Community Centre became known in East Wall as the Swiss Cheese.

Outside the OPW, in a parallel world, things were on the move. *Making a Modern Street*, held under the umbrella of the Independent Artists at the Hugh Lane Gallery, was Dublin's first group exhibition of architectural models and drawings, intentionally aimed at developing a new audience for architecture. I began teaching after office hours in the studios at UCD. We worked in collaboration with students and teaching colleagues, in opposition to mono-functional office blocks, in favour of multi-use residential buildings. *In Dublin* magazine published some alternative urban projects and they were presented for discussion on RTÉ's *Live Arts Show*. We opened an architecture gallery, the Blue Studio, a high space on Dawson Street, rent-free, courtesy of de Blacam and Meagher. The City Architecture Studio presented *Projects for the Liffey Quays* at the Blue Studio, to illustrate the potential for ten thousand people to live in the vacant docklands. That exhibition was reviewed in the UK, published on the cover of the *Architects' Journal*. Such speculative work, together with a handful of buildings on site, led to an invitation for a group exhibition at the Architectural Association in London. The *Figurative Architecture* exhibition transferred directly from the AA to l'Institut Français d'Architecture in Paris, then back to the Hugh Lane Gallery in Dublin.

Arranging that exhibition and editing its catalogue got me on to speaking terms with Alvin Boyarsky, the inspirational leader of the AA School, inventor of the so-called 'unit system' that gave young teachers the scope to work out their positions, learning-by-doing in step with their students. He later invited me to join his panel of external examiners, a position I enjoyed for six or seven years, the last few visits as chair of the board of examiners. Boyarsky loved books, loved making books that were made to express the ethos of the architecture under discussion, books as objects in themselves. He sometimes asked me into his office to look at new books in preparation for publication, to smell the paper: 'Does it feel cheap enough? I've paid a lot for this effect.' I mentioned that his newly published folio on the demanding Swedish architect Sigurd Lewerentz, with its rough sandpaper cover, would rip the surface from other books beside it on my bookshelf. 'Don't you think that's what Lewerentz would have wanted?' At the AA, I made new and lasting friends in architectural education and critical practice, an eye-opener for me in many ways and refreshing for my teaching activities in Dublin.

On my return to Dublin, I had joined the committee of the Architectural Association of Ireland, a voluntary group of enthusiasts for the proliferation of architectural culture. I started by organising lectures and exhibitions, and was elected president after a number of years' active service on the committee. One lasting contribution that I can lay claim to in this arena, one of a number of efforts to increase public interest in the appreciation of architecture, would be the initiation of the AAI Awards in 1986, still going strong as an annual indicator of emerging ideas in Irish architecture, its rules unchanged, its energies undimmed. It was established as a travelling exhibition, first hosted at the Taylor Galleries, then touring to other arts venues around the country, and continued to attract significant support and substantial funding from the Arts Council for many years, an early sign of the Council's commitment to recognising architecture as an artistic practice.

In my capacity as an AAI committee member, in the autumn of 1981 I was able to invite James Stirling to deliver a public lecture in Dublin on his recent work, a lecture with a special emphasis on the Stuttgart gallery, its concrete structure almost complete, still in the raw, looking like a noble ruin, before it ended up getting buttered all over in bands of stone. The lure that persuaded Stirling to accept such an invitation, describing unfinished buildings not being his usual practice, was that an outing could be arranged to visit Lutyens's work on Lambay Island. In 1904, Edwin Lutyens, already established as an architect of Arts and Crafts houses very closely connected to their gardens, not yet caught up in his later captivation with the 'high game' of the classical style, had been commissioned for an unlikely project. He had been invited to take on the conversion of an empty island, its ruined castle and outlying cowsheds, as a country estate, a lovers' hideaway, an out-of-town retreat for a wealthy London banker and his new wife, an American divorcée and well-known society beauty. This was to become a labour of love for Lutyens, keeping him involved with every detail of the work, house and garden, returning him to the island every summer for thirty years.

From a distance, glimpsed from the window of planes coming into land at Dublin Airport, only partly revealed in publications of Lutyens's work, the most compelling aspect of the scheme is its encircling rampart wall, three hundred metres in diameter, an elevated wall walk with the medieval castle at the pivot point of the plan. The circular enclosure provides wind shelter for trees to grow, lawns and terraces, a paradise garden in an otherwise windswept and bare rocky island landscape. This much was known before we set foot on the island. What had not been expected was the architectural complexity and aesthetic integrity of the castle interior.

It was a tricky trip to organise, there being no telephone on the island, with only radio contact via the Baily Lighthouse on Howth Head. The old island boat, the *Shamrock*, was damaged in a sudden storm just days before the planned visit. Another boat and boatman had to be found at short notice. It was a basic fishing boat, barely seaworthy, lacking in luxuries like seating, with large gaps in the decking and a sputtering engine. Stirling, recently recovered from a serious illness, was to fly out of Dublin to Washington to pick up the Pritzker Prize the following day. He began to worry as soon as we boarded the boat, when the boatman wound up his alarm clock, set it to ring at the turn of the tide, muttering warnings of chancy currents and the hazards of being stranded on the Malahide sandbar.

Tensions eased as soon as we walked through the wooden gate in the circular wall and onto the greener-than-green stone-edged grassy path through the woodland garden. A formal landscape design inscribed onto the natural form of the island. And islanded within that wider boundary wall, further isolated from their wild surroundings, lay the inner courtyards that Lutyens had arranged around the renewed shell of the angled castle walls. Lord Revelstoke, son of the original clients, strolled down the hill to meet us, breathing vapours of gin into the clear morning air. Revelstoke had reverentially maintained each aspect of the house exactly as his parents left it, their remains respectfully interred in the Lutyens-designed memorial in the outer wall, both buried under one word carved in stone, 'QUIET'. Every linen-covered couch, hinged window curtain, wooden chair and folding table held in place as if, in this place, for now, time itself stood still.

And so, somehow, magically, the whole place survives intact to this day, its ethos closely guarded by two of the first clients' great-grandchildren. All these undisturbed artefacts add to the Arts and Crafts atmosphere, but the real wonders of Lambay Castle are the space-shaping moments and inventive possibilities developed by Lutyens in response to the irregularities of the medieval structure. Twisting stone stairs, hovering timber platforms, inside-outside passageways, and the marvellously mountainous roof swoops of the kitchen court. At the foot of the turning limestone stair, standing still, not moving a muscle, suspended in an out-of-body psycho-spatial sensation, you feel drawn to move in two directions at once, your left eye leading you up onto the dark landings, your right eye pulling you down a passage towards the brightly daylit kitchen court.

Revelstoke took something of a shine to Stirling, especially when he admired the bay-windowed northern elevation for its romantic picturesque composition. 'Romantic', 'picturesque', the very words noted by the man he remembered as 'Uncle Ned' on his pencil sketches for that bulging extension to the ruined side of the castle. 'Let me show you the drawings. Do you mind if I call you Sir James?' asked the impressed lord. 'Not at all!' replied the as-yet unknighted architect. It took quite a struggle to pull Stirling out of his reverie with his newfound friend Revelstoke, reminding him that he had a plane to catch, a prize to receive, the Pritzker Prize to be passed into his hands by Philip Johnson tomorrow afternoon. 'Johnson will be jealous when I tell him what I've seen today,' he chuckled, looking forward to having one up on the man who had everything. Stirling would be dining out on his discovery of Lambay for years to come, still waxing about the wind-bent trees when we met for the last time at the opening of his Venice Biennale bookshop in 1991.

Dublin in the 1980s is remembered as a time when many were leaving, when times were bad. From our perspective, starting out, here to stay, it was an interesting time to be alive, to be socially engaged. New things were happening, restless signs spread through the city, omens of promise across the culture. Fuelled by energies instilled in the 1970s, we were determined to drive through the depression, to campaign, to live a changed life from the sex-segregated limits of our parents' generation. Lines were drawn in the campaign against the Eighth Amendment referendum in 1983. Things were going to be different. We felt ourselves connected in a cultural shift.

We got married in the Registry Office, a civil ceremony then becoming almost acceptably normal in liberal Dublin society, not yet so well recognised beyond the city limits. It was a point of principle with us to hold out against religious conformity; we didn't need the blessing of any church, but, being conventional souls, determined atheists still religious in disposition, we wanted some public expression of a social commitment, a civic celebration. My mother coped with the unprecedented situation by insisting that all the Tuomey women wore hats, church or no church. Sheila's parents hosted a garden party. And that fine summer's day went smoothly.

We bought a house in a quiet street in Broadstone, its structure undisturbed by any changes in character since it was built one hundred and fifty years before; shutter-boxes, stair-hall, fireplaces and outhouse all survived intact. Two storeys over half-basement, granite steps up to the front door, a typical Dublin terraced house. We opened up the upper floors, turned a six-roomed house into a four-roomed house, kitchen in the middle, bedrooms below in the basement, living space upstairs, an upside-down house, London style.

Dublin, its centre being compact, was still a walkable city, and, its terrain being level in the main, an easily cyclable city. The city-encircled bay, the stone-walled Liffey quays. Dublin is sliced in two and at the same time unified by the line of the Liffey. The river slides through from west to east, stoppered at one end by the open space of the Phoenix Park, open-mouthed at the other end to the wide Irish Sea. A swim in the sea within daily reach, a walk in the mountains at the weekend. Dublin may be flat, but it is not formless. The legible geography of its Georgian brick street pattern, low parapets, and consequently big skies. Salt air and sea gulls. A low-key, unspectacular skyline. The city lands have long since spread out loosely and unchecked to the west and north, with car-driving commuters daily disappearing out of view into the outer space of the soul-devouring suburbs. Downtown living was affordable at that point in Dublin's development, its comparative lack of development.

We bought a car, an old Citroën, and learned to drive. At the weekends, we would drive out of Dublin, into the landscape with a paperback copy of Maurice Craig's *Ireland Observed* as our guide. We wanted to explore the vernacular background of schools, barns, handball alleys, water towers, sea pools, a Quixotic quest for the lost or hidden soul of Irish architecture. A pointless search, probably, but one that taught us a more attentive way of looking. We were seeking a subject, some connection to a collective memory, a purpose for ourselves, what we all want to find, our place in the world.

And so, little by little, we settled into life in the city.

Through the 1980s, Irish theatre played an emancipatory part in our lives, energising our outlook, similar in its effect to the European cinema of the 1970s. The films of Francesco Rosi – *Christ Stopped at Eboli*,

Three Brothers – had shown us beautiful whitewashed space–volume structures, suggesting our spiritual home might be in Italy. These new plays recast Irish life in word–image scenes that made us see our true home landscape with fresh eyes. Irish life enacted, made real, made new, like in the movies, only rarely revealed in Irish cinema for some reason, not much of it seen between Neil Jordan's haunting *Angel* and Colm Bairéad's recent and beautiful *An Cailín Ciúin*. I should list those plays as experienced, in chronological order, not that such things matter, except, I suppose, in hindsight.

I saw Brian Friel's classic, *Faith Healer*, at the Abbey in September 1980, while I was planning my return to Dublin, shortly after my interview at the OPW. This memory play, hoping for a miracle, diminishing into disappointment, was not set in Ireland in the main. It was based in British provincial backwaters, made familiar to its Dublin audience by minimal staging, suggesting the backyard of any Irish bar. It ended up, and sadly, in a backyard in Donegal. I hold on to the image of Donal McCann playing Frank Hardy, walking downstage in front of a huge banner, hands held high in the air, skipping along between imagined parents, and, as he dropped his arms, changing scale without changing size. He turned from a child to a man, a miracle performed by the faith-healing actor in a few short strides.

Later that season, at the Dublin Theatre Festival, *Translations*, a second Friel masterwork, played at the Gate. When Hugh the hedge-school master told the English lieutenant, 'We feel closer to the warm Mediterranean. We tend to overlook your little island,' there was a sudden eruption out of the audience, newly united in a burst of applause for Ray McAnally's aplomb, a collective expression of post colonial relief. The play was telling us, we who had grown up with Wordsworth in our heads, that we were all Europeans now. In May 2011, the day of the opening of our building for the Lyric Theatre in Belfast, one of the days of my life as an architect, Brian Friel stood on the new stage to call down a litany of secular blessings, that the new building would be 'a warm house, a welcoming house, a sacred place, a house of play, because a solemn theatre is a dead theatre'. *Translations* played at the Lyric, to appreciative audiences once again, in May 2022, dynamically staged in a diagonal setting.

Back then, three years later in 1983, downstairs at the Peacock, we saw *The Great Hunger* adapted from the long poem of Patrick Kavanagh, Tom MacIntyre's collaboration with director Patrick Mason and actor Tom Hickey. In this radically visual production, the actors wore corduroy trousers, the stage floor was a ploughed field, the backdrop lined with corrugated iron, the whole scene scaled in a variety of ridges and furrows. I had the nerve to jump to my feet at the finish, shouting 'Bravo!'

> Sitting on a wooden gate,
> Sitting on a wooden gate,
> Sitting on a wooden gate
> He didn't care a damn.

Said whatever came into his head,
Said whatever came into his head,
Said whatever came into his head
And inconsequently sang.

And along came *The Gigli Concert*, upstairs at the Abbey,
Patrick Mason directing another electric performance
from Tom Hickey. A city-based play by Tom Murphy, no
rural backdrop, the scattered interior of an upstairs flat.
A week in the life of a dynamatolgist, a hoaxer–miracle
worker, like Friel's faith healer, but this time to conclusively
positive effect. The moment where Hickey mimed God
running Adam and Eve right out of the Garden of Eden,
was a cathartic piece of stage magic.

Bertolt Brecht's advice to his actors – 'Show the course
of your work to the audience … they are standing not only
in front of your work but also in the world' – reminds me
of how these theatrical inspirations affected our idea of
architectural communication. Architecture is the theatre of
the city. It makes space for the purposes it is built to house
and, at the same time, as it adapts to changes over time,
stands open to the life of the world.

Each of these plays, written by elderly playwrights, or
elderly by our standards then, each of them being aged
about fifty, was telling us that something was happening
and instructing us to be alert to the change. The night
before our second son was born, we went to see *Too Late
for Logic* at the Abbey. It might not have been Murphy's
best play, but the title was timely for us.

When the children arrived, two sons born four years apart, everything changed. Grown-up life started again with the gift of these two new lives. Apart from the biological phenomena of childbearing – pregnancy, birth, breastfeeding we aimed to share all other aspects of childrearing. We worked, cooked, cleaned and played in equal measure, with no separation of roles. We were, as Sheila's father used to say, 'blessed with those boys!' Lucky for us. Our world was enriched, nothing lost, everything gained. The boys went out to crèche, nursery, preschool. Four of us went off to work in the morning and met again in the evening, a family on a mission, as our younger son recalls. Was it Louis Kahn who said the place for the child is under the table? Sheila kept a big cardboard box under her drawing desk, where the baby played away. Our first office was a room with the most glamorous view in Dublin, four floors up a stone spiral stair, overlooking the fulcrum of College Green. Travelling to teach in America, where I had been visiting critic at Princeton and Harvard, was curtailed after two years in favour of spending time with the boys. No more nights wasted in open-ended arguments, theorising in the pubs off Grafton Street. No more late nights dining at Nico's or dancing at Sides. No more late-night weekends at the drawing board. Not for a while.

We moved from our eyrie on College Green to rent an old schoolhouse building on Camden Row, a high-windowed studio that has served as our base of operations for more than thirty years. A lucky find, a home from home, an empty white space that filled up slowly. Crowded now with colleagues busy at their work, silently populated by stacked folios of drawings and shelves of models, evidence of exhibitions installed and designs under way, buildings built and unbuilt, projects lost and won.

Many of those involved in the 1980s decade of collaborative ventures teamed up together again as Group 91, this time to do something concrete and practical for Dublin's turn as European City of Culture in 1991. And that, in turn, is what led to the big breakthrough for our collective enterprise, the competition-winning scheme for the urban regeneration of Temple Bar.

And by that time, around the beginning of the 1990s, the point at which this part of my story closes, a new kind of optimism was in the ether. Mary Robinson had been elected as President of Ireland, the first woman president, a sophisticated feminist, and outward-looking. Charles Haughey, as leader of the opposition and in-and-out Taoiseach, had been manoeuvred into supporting the arts-led campaign to save Temple Bar from the threat of demolition and the curse of comprehensive development. We were already on site with the Irish Film Centre, now known as the IFI, an amalgam of film societies, film archive, arthouse screens, education outreach and cinema-related activities. It was to become the pilot project for the Temple Bar regeneration. The concept of the 'cultural cluster', synergies tested out at the Film Centre, became a strategic vehicle, and an effective one, for attracting European regional development funding. At that moment, short-lived as it turned out to be, and despite the scandals of the day, there was a widely shared feeling of hope, a shaky but beguiling belief in the idea of positive progress in the world. European integration, women's liberation, the fall of the Berlin Wall, Mandela out of jail, the prospect of an end to fighting in Ireland after the Anglo-Irish Agreement, the end of history, the chance was being offered of better times ahead.

We were lucky to have started our practice with two 'public' projects, commissions that arose not from entering competitions but out of our engagement with the world of film, theatre and education. 'Public' is here placed in inverted commas, because the long string of feasibility studies that led to building the Irish Film Centre and the Ranelagh Multi-Denominational School came about out of activism, volunteering as part of a movement, professional skills offered to develop briefs, test sites. If these were personal commissions, the personal was political. This is different in every way from the present predicament for architects seeking public work, with all of the emphasis on prequalification criteria and restrictive procedures, with avenues of access firmly closed to those who have never done it before. So many of Dublin's best buildings have been done by first-timers, brand new starters; Edward Lovett Pearce's Parliament Building in College Green, Paul Koralek's Berkeley Library at Trinity College, Andrzej Wejchert's master plan for UCD's Belfield Campus. Each of these architects was aged just twenty-seven when they landed those jobs. The Royal Institute of the Architects of

Ireland has awarded twenty-four Triennial Gold Medals, regarded as the highest award for a building in Irish architecture. The average age of the gold-medal winning architects, crucially, their age at the date of commission, stands at thirty-seven, the majority having had no track record in the winning building category. The lesson might be that if you want the best school, theatre, library, whatever, you should ask a young architect who's never done it before. Nobody concentrates like a beginner.

The night the Irish Film Centre opened its doors, as we raised a glass in the bar with friends after the screening of Stephen Gyllenhaal's ghostly, patchy *Waterland*, we had the feeling of standing on a ledge, ready for lift-off. September 1992, our first public building, a packed house, a public space, open to the city, approached from four directions, north, south, east and west, through narrow lanes and passageways, a secret place rediscovered. There was, as they say, something in the air that night, excitement, confidence in the culture, a sense of things opening up. We had tasted something akin to this in the summer of 1991 with our very first building project, albeit a temporary one.

This was the so-called Irish Pavilion, a studio–gallery purpose-designed for twelve paintings, a red corrugated iron shed parked at an awkward angle in the courtyard of the Irish Museum of Modern Art. This pavilion, developed in collaboration with the painter Brian Maguire, had emerged from an artist–architect blind-pairing selection process, painter and architect working together, raising funds and persuading sponsors to help us on our way to the *11 Cities, 11 Nations: Contemporary Nordic Art and Architecture* exhibition held in the Netherlands. The pavilion was re-erected outdoors for the opening of IMMA, where it stood askew in the candy quadrangle for six weeks. It provoked some strong responses. It was more popular with artists than with architects. By and large it was hated by the press, condemned as a rude intrusion into the historic setting of the Royal Hospital Kilmainham. We were, admittedly, a little wounded, but in our hearts we believed it might mark the new beginning we were looking for, an expressive structure appropriate to its purpose, drawing on the poignancy of the vernacular, staking a claim for character in architecture.

The reception for the Film Centre was much less complicated. Our work here was widely welcomed, as if the city had been waiting for something new-into-old, transformative of the given conditions of the historical city. Something lasting. It has since passed the test of time, a courtyard hollowed out of the city block, daylit from a sawtooth glass roof, like a railway station. It has suffered a few rude changes, some major and many minor. Slightly injured but substantially the same, it survives as a meeting place in the city.

That busy year, with the emotional contrast between the birth pains of the long-gone Pavilion, itself a consciously disruptive installation, in critical conversation with its surroundings, fitting in by standing out, and the IFI's almost instantaneous assimilation into its urban background, a healing intervention in a difficult context, that year was the push that got us started on the path of our work life to come.

This is the story of my upbringing, my beginnings, my inner outlook, before my outer life developed as a working architect, an outline of events from the twenty-five years before my collaboration with Sheila really got me going, before we settled into life in Dublin and began to put down roots in Connemara. A Japanese friend once told me, back in the London days, meaning it as a compliment, I feel sure, that my student portfolio was 'already beyond'. I can't say how the places passed through in my youth have made me what I am, or exactly how those experiences have shaped my horizon. They seem to be left behind, far away in another time, another place. I have moved on, in that sense 'already beyond'. I don't feel I belong within any of the social landscapes of my upbringing, no community ties to locale, no townland of origin, no childhood home territory, except in my memory, except in my head, in my mind's eye, where all these place–time connections remain real and alive.

This story is not going to run out into a career summary. My lucky life in architecture is well documented, project by project. I've written elsewhere about buildings built, big and small. Ideas live in the work. An architect's thoughts are transferred from first sketches into models and working drawings, carried across into construction, translated into the material world. And the buildings are there to speak for themselves, even if some would be forced to tell stories of frustration and failure. The architect isn't needed to stand by on street corners and explain. Buildings last a long time, longer than our human lifespan. They belong in the world. Once they're up and ready, as far as their architect-author is concerned, they are as they must be, 'already beyond'. Their secret conversation, silent but intense, goes on forever; house to house, void to shell, building to building, down all the days.

Looking Out

And when you're in the bigger room
You might not know what to do
You might have to think of how it all got started
Sitting in your little room
The White Stripes, 'Little Room'

I'M GAZING OUT OF the window, wondering where the days have gone, how things have changed since the future lay far out in front of me. Will there be a time when we get to the point of arrival, instead of pursuing what's just around the corner? I am lucky enough to be busy with the sort of work I would have hoped for when I was young. Busy at home and abroad; that is, if you can call England abroad. On a childhood holiday in the Aran Islands, a jarvey man once asked me, 'How are the potatoes with ye abroad in Galway?' I grew up with the idea, influenced by my parents, teachers and mentors, that it's best to make yourself useful and that, if you concentrate your efforts on the work at hand, it might be possible to make a lasting contribution. Useful beauty. That's the dream, and that much hasn't changed. On it goes, no sign of stopping.

The world outside has changed. I grew up in an age of promise and possibility. To make any kind of architecture, an optimistic outlook is essential. It's a basic requirement of our profession, a necessary position to maintain against the fractured condition and threatened futurity of the world.

To contribute to the shape of society, to accommodate its institutions both spatial and social, calls for a positive commitment of mind, a belief that ideas can be enshrined in the physical structure of buildings. Is it futile to propose a fine house in a shattered neighbourhood? If you can't control everything, is it folly to try to control anything? It seems to me that the architect has to answer in the affirmative. When faced with this question, the problem of the world gone wrong, Alvar Aalto said, 'You can't change the world, you can only set it an example.' I live by this maxim still.

Dublin has changed, the context has shifted. The attraction of the run-down city of my youth, for those with an appetite for change, was that everything appeared to be possible. The delirious potentiality of a derelict site. A vacant site, an open city, the locus of multiple possibilities. But as soon as a plot has been poorly constructed, and almost every empty corner has now been developed, with one banal, bad and boring building after another, the flicker of hope is on the wane. The promise of many small flames has been put out all over the city. A further problem of extinguished potentiality is that buildings supposedly designed to last twenty years are most likely to survive for a century, though many may deserve to be knocked down after less than a decade. This is too pessimistic a prospect to contemplate, even if it's true for the most part. In a properly adjusted world, no buildings should be easily demolished. The city should be built to endure, to be adaptable to change and to weather with age.

It's better to see the urban organism *en bloc*, through half-closed eyes, as a built thing in itself, to understand the whole city as a conglomerate construction. The human achievement of the inherited landscape is worth holding on to, layers of accumulation waiting to be discovered, and once properly understood, all of it susceptible to new interpretation, open to renewal and change. The renowned historian John Summerson, author of *Georgian London*, a very fine book, did Georgian Dublin a serious disservice, and his own reputation too, long ago in the 1960s, when he condemned a run of sixteen houses on Fitzwilliam Street to summary execution. 'One damned house after another,' he arrogantly declared. And, taking licence from this expert adjudication, acting in the interests of the State, the Electricity Supply Board knocked them all down. And, shame to say, this wilful destruction was supported by some vocal architecture students at the time. They might be forgiven for their haste, for their youth, desperate as they must have been for signs of change in a stifled situation. But Summerson should have known better. He misread the character of Dublin's streetscape, judging it lacking in the compositional coherence of London's squares, their terraces designed as elevational set pieces, centre blocks complete with side-wing pavilions. He was blind to the accretional beauties of Dublin's stuttering pattern of development, two or three houses built together at a time, nudging up against their neighbours, never exactly the same, working together in a syncopated rhythm, maintaining an uneven continuity of urban form.

Five years after the ill-advised interruption of Fitzwilliam Street's so-called Georgian mile, a new generation of architecture students led a semi-successful protest against the demolition of four houses on the corner of Hume Street and Stephen's Green. The Hume Street protest helped raise public awareness, which was a good thing, but the resulting compromise of a bog-standard office block masked by a mere facsimile façade was no substitute for the real thing. 'Queen Anne in front and Mary Ann behind.' Then, five years later, the Pembroke Street occupation successfully prevented Bord na Móna destroying a fine row of five houses. Nowadays, since those student-led occupations helped to turn the tide, Dublin's Georgian houses might be considered safe in the main, over-protected some might say, but certainly under-used. They need to be lived in again. To survive alive, any organism has to remain open to change.

Meantime, many sensible and silent buildings of the 1970s, structures capable of conversion to multi-use activity, are being needlessly knocked, scoured out and discarded before they could come of age. And down in the newly developed docklands, despite the chance offered by extensive changes in configuration, the chemistry doesn't convince, there's an insufficient stimulus for multivalent vitality. Convivial life has not been awakened in this neutral environment, in this over-shiny and under-inhabited twilight zone.

All is not lost; the city fabric remains physically intact. The city centre is cosily contained between the bent arms of two canals, the Royal and the Grand, working waterways no more, the functional landscape of their stone-lined infrastructure having proved beautifully adaptable as linear parkways. The canals hold the mental map of the city in shape. But much of the core, so well defined, stands sadly empty of the sounds of ordinary life. Dublin's elegant streets echo by night and at weekends like hollow shells. Vacant upper floors lack the warmth that comes from lights on after dark. Something must be done to save the situation. It's not difficult to imagine a liveable city, easy to remember living cities seen elsewhere, but there is little local progress to report, not yet, not enough, not nearly enough.

Slipping down stone stairs into mysterious basements was a condition of emergence into independent life for me as a student. Where better to experience the flavour of underground activity? From my first nervous ventures into the folk club scene in Parnell Square, to regular Saturday afternoon attendance at Supply, Demand and Curve's moody concerts in some gloomy basement in Abbey Street. Even the conservative Country Shop café was entered through a basement. I went to meetings of the Living City Group, small gatherings held in a basement flat in Fitzwilliam Street, an early source of education in the social architecture of city life. At the same time, probably during my second year in college, I turned up for meetings in another stone-flagged basement kitchen, this one in Percy Place, where group discussions focused on setting up a deinstitutionalised university, all classes to be distributed in vacant rooms, upstairs as well as downstairs, across the city. Inspired by these sessions, I went to hear Ivan Illich address a packed-out lecture theatre in Belfield. He was travelling the world, university to university, proclaiming the case for *Deschooling Society*, arguing for a locally based, village like lifestyle, with no need for anybody to travel further than twelve miles. Illich was intense, his writing had been instructive to read, but here he stood at the lectern, admonishing us in the flesh, off-puttingly fixated in his views, probably jet-lagged from the never-ending lecture circuit. His appeal for society to slow down and restructure seemed contradictory to his own practice and consequently diminished in its powers of persuasion. The shine had worn off.

I've been thinking about these basement beginnings. Places apart, disconnected from life above ground. They have not lost their lustre. I began my studies in the basement studios of Earlsfort Terrace, lived in basement flats when I first went to London, worked in the basement of Stirling's office. The house I live in now, like every house in the street, like almost every house in the historic core, sits sunken in a semi-basement courtyard garden. None of these basement areas were dug out like trenches, even if it seems that way. The reverse is the case. It's the street that's been raised above the natural grade. One of the unsung wonders of the Georgian city-building system is the energy invested in its extensive manipulations of surrounding ground levels. 'Streets in the air!' was the mid-twentieth-century slogan that sought to replicate the traditional street in the form of access decks to multi-storey apartments. But streets in the air were not a new idea. Re-levelling the landscape is the basic premise of the terraced house. A terraced landscape underlies every terrace of houses. Sewers and services, coal-holes and cellars lie embedded below the pavement. When you step out from your doorstep to walk on the footpath, the common ground connecting house and town, you are unconsciously interacting with the infrastructure. Basements are the subliminal baseline of the city. Most of the time, the invisible architecture of this great civic invention goes unnoticed. 'I have often walked down this street before, but the pavement always stayed beneath my feet before.'

Dublin is my home town now. I've lived here for forty-five years, thirty of them in this terraced house, where I'm looking out of the window at a calp stone wall, the stolid rear of the Rathmines dome. The house has been subjected to several phases of change in what's getting close to its two-hundred-year history. It started out as one integrated half of a double-fronted house. But it soon got divided off. Somebody sliced through the original plan after only twenty years. Bolted a hall and stair onto the freshly opened side to heal the wound. This explains the curious position of two crucial chimney stacks standing inboard at the centre of a standard late-Georgian plan, instead of stabilising the structure of the party wall like chimneys are supposed to do. Later, it was brutally subdivided into substandard flats, losing one stair, three fireplaces and many superficial details in the process. Then, just as soon as we moved in, by our own design, its centre was voided out to make a double height volume, one room subtracted to open the house towards the garden. Further instability, wilfully inflicted. Over the past thirty years, a typical plan has been steadily reworked through repairs and alterations, to implant or uncover moments of atypicality within the type. Now, nearly finished, there's a new studio at the end of the garden, a long-term plan so that we never have to stop work, no matter what happens in the ups and downs of professional practice.

We are wedded to the idea of the studio workplace, the idea of studio life, the environment where we met as students, the world of our teaching and practice. We bought this house because it faced a back lane with an empty site, the location where once might have been, but never was, as far as old maps can tell us, a stable or a mews. We wanted to complete the site plan, provide a destination at the foot of the garden. When our sons were small, they played at the muddy end. Then it became a dump. I was told by a forgiving gardener that every garden needs a dump. I'm not much of a gardener, though I like planting trees. Displacing the disused muddy end and the over-scaled dump, we've designed a simple rectangular plan with an irregular bite taken out of it, and a garden to protect the roots of two birch trees planted when first we put down roots in this plot. Nothing as grandiose as the end-of-garden campanile Francis Johnston built behind his early nineteenth-century house on Eccles Street, a full-scale steeple, complete with ringing bells until the neighbours complained, perhaps a personal study or private memento for his marvellously public spire for St George's Church on Hardwicke Place. Ours is a shed-like structure, a sloping roof to protect our view to the dome, mono-pitched over a single if slightly complex volume, creating two negative spaces, side garden and sunken court, exploiting the difference in level between street and lane. A long-awaited addition to a long-suffering, perfectly ordinary and endlessly adaptable house.

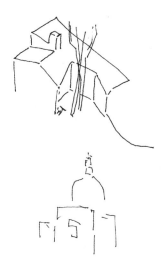

I love the busy downtown cores of solid-block cities, where streets run smoothly into each other at crossroads with no discernible break in spatial containment. Carved-out streams of space converging, like you'd find in Rome and Venice, passageways narrowing down to tight dimensions and widening out into room-like pools for social gathering. On the opposite extreme, far from city life, I love the focusing presence of settlements in rural surroundings. What visual comfort would the sea give if it had no pier to hit, or had we no headland to measure its vast horizon? The mountains that I enjoy, to paraphrase the late Luigi Snozzi, a Swiss mountain-dwelling urbanist of many aphorisms, are the ones where I know there's a town or village on the other side. A farmhouse folded into a hillside is better by far from my point of view than any unworked landscape. Powerfully imprinted on my inner eye are those places where geology seems to anticipate human construction, the cathedral-like space of the red-rock Canyon de Chelly, the street-like stepped-back profile of Aran's Atlantic cliffs, glacial valleys and carved-out limestone platforms, where natural formations are analogous to architectural form.

I grew up close to building sites, learned to draw on the back of engineering blueprints. My ambidextrous father, having been forced to learn to write with his right hand, left hand held behind his back, could work his way across an elephant-size engineering drawing, the pen changing hands midway, the lettering staying consistent in style and slant from side to side. He taught me, showed me, the satisfaction of paying attention to the discipline, how to sit at a desk and draw. No sinister supervisor prevented me from using my left hand. I was encouraged to communicate through diagrams, learned how to bisect an angle, to understand the square on the hypotenuse, to survey complicated field shapes with ranging rods, dumpy level and telescopic staff, and how to join the jumbled dots of spot levels, to transform random-seeming data into flowing contour lines. Vasari, author of *The Lives of the Artists*, tells the story of Giotto's circle, how the maestro, when asked by a messenger to send an example of his work to the patron Pope, demonstrated his mastery by strapping one arm to his side, and, 'with a turn of his hand', drew a perfect circle in a single sweep. I've never been much of a master-maker myself, neither craft-skilled nor hands-on, but, through concept and design, from first thought to final detail, I have relished every chance to participate in the energy of things being made for a purpose.

I work things out in my head, in my bed, in my notebook, on my bicycle. I like drawing lines and seeing those lines clearly drawn again in the ground and appearing in the air. I like folded outlines, faceted forms, offset and balanced volumes, angled skylines and chamfered corners. Not too straight and nothing too simple, the resultant form showing that it's come through a hardening process of approximation and reduction before taking shape in material reality. And I like the vocabulary of in-between spaces, porches, verandas, overhangs and ledges, sheltering places brought to life by shafts of sunlight and sheets of rain.

If I had no work of my own to do, no more buildings to design or to build, I hope I'd be kept busy with the appreciation of spaces and in the observation of things, exploring the mysteries of strange and familiar places and the range of ideas embodied in interesting buildings, old and new, happy to be an architect with eyes to see and hands to draw.

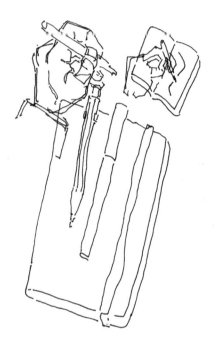

Acknowledgments

To readers and listeners who offered encouragement and advice: Clíodhna Ní Anluain, Eimear Arthur, Anne Enright, Martin Hayes, Niall Hobhouse, Ellen Rowley, Billie Tsien, Shane O'Toole, Peter Walsh.

'Far from Home': first draft read on RTÉ *Sunday Miscellany*, 10 July 2022.

'Ten Years' Time': first draft read at 'Architecture and Its Stories', AIARG Conference; 25 March 2022.

'Learning from Stirling': first draft published on drawingmatter.org; 15 June 2020.

Arnold, Eddy and Cindy Walker, 'You Don't Know Me' (Mijac Music: 1955). All rights reserved. Courtesy of Carlin Music Delaware LLC, Clearwater Yard, 35 Inverness Street, London, NW1 7HB.

Dylan, Bob, 'My Back Pages' (1964); 'I Dreamed I Saw St Augustine' (1967) (Universal Tunes). Reprinted by permission of Hal Leonard Europe Ltd.

Eliot, T. S, 'The Love Song of J. Alfred Prufrock', *Prufrock and Other Observations* (Faber & Faber: London, 1917).

Friel, Brian, *Translations* (Faber & Faber: London, 1980).

Heaney, Seamus, *District and Circle* (Faber & Faber: London, 2006).

Homer, trans. Robert Fagles, *The Odyssey* (Penguin Random House: London, 2006).

Jacobsen, Roy, trans. Don Bartlett and Don Shaw, *The Unseen* (Quercus Editions: London, 2017). Reproduced with permission of the licensor through PLSclear.

Kavanagh, Patrick, 'The Great Hunger', *Collected Poems*, ed. Antoinette Quinn (Allen Lane: London 2004). By kind permission of the Trustees of the Estate of the late Katherine B. Kavanagh through the Jonathan Williams Literary Agency.

Lennon, John and Paul McCartney, 'In My Life' (1965); 'With a Little Help from My Friends' (1967) (Sony Music Publishing). Reprinted by permission of Hal Leonard Europe Ltd.

Stendhal, *The Life of Henry Brulard* (Penguin Random House: London, 1995).

Stirling, James, 'An Architect's Approach to Architecture', *RIBA Journal*, May 1965.

The White Stripes, 'Little Room' (Peppermint Stripe Music, 2001). Reprinted by permission of Hal Leonard Europe Ltd.

O'Donnell + Tuomey: Selected Works 1991–2025

1991 Irish Pavilion, Irish Museum of Modern Art, Kilmainham, Dublin, Ireland

1992 Irish Film Institute, Temple Bar, Dublin, Ireland

1994 Blackwood Golf Centre, Clandeboye, Co. Down, Northern Ireland

1996 Gallery of Photography, Temple Bar, Dublin, Ireland

1996 National Photographic Archive / School of Photography, Temple Bar, Dublin, Ireland

1998 Ranelagh Multidenominational School, Dublin, Ireland

2002 Furniture College, Letterfrack, Co. Galway, Ireland

2002 Press Reception Room, Leinster House, Dublin, Ireland

2002 Social Housing, Galbally, Co. Limerick, Ireland

2003 Centre for Research into Infectious Diseases, University College Dublin, Ireland

2004 *Transformation of an Institution*, Ireland's Pavilion, Venice Biennale, Venice, Italy

2004 Glucksman Gallery, University College Cork, Ireland

2006 Cherry Orchard School, Dublin, Ireland

2007 Irish Art Research Centre, Provost's Stables, Trinity College Dublin, Ireland

2008 Seán O'Casey Community Centre, East Wall, Dublin, Ireland

2008 *The Lives of Spaces* (group show), Ireland's Pavilion, Venice Biennale, Venice, Italy

2009 Irish Language Cultural Centre, Derry, Northern Ireland

2009 Timberyard Social Housing, Cork Street, Dublin, Ireland

2011 Lyric Theatre, Belfast, Northern Ireland

2012 The Photographers' Gallery, Soho, London, UK

2012 *Vessel*, Venice Biennale, installation in International Show, Venice, Italy

2014 Saw Swee Hock Student Centre, London School of Economics, London, UK

2016 St. Angela's College, Cork, Ireland

2016 Central European University, Budapest, Hungary

2018 *Folding Landscapes*, Venice Biennale, installation in International Show, Venice, Italy

2018 Cavanagh Bridge, University College Cork, Ireland

2019 Sandford Park School, Dublin, Ireland

2019 Student Hub, University College Cork, Ireland

2022 Passage House, Joseph Walsh Studio, Co. Cork, Ireland

2023 Stone Vessel, Joseph Walsh Studio, Co. Cork, Ireland

2024   Academic Hub and Library, Technological University Dublin, Ireland

2024   School of Architecture, University of Liverpool, Liverpool, UK

2024   Sadler's Wells Dance Theatre and Studios, Stratford Waterfront, London, UK

2025   Victoria & Albert East Museum, Stratford Waterfront, London, UK

O'Donnell + Tuomey have been selected for more than 130 national and international awards over the past thirty-five years. Seven times winner of the AAI Downes Medal. Six times shortlisted for the EU Mies Award. Five times finalist for the RIBA Stirling Prize. Three times shortlisted for the RIBA International Prize. Twice winners of RIAI Triennial Gold Medals 2005 and 2021. Recipient of two lifetime achievement awards: American Academy of Arts and Letters Brunner Prize 2015 and RIBA Royal Gold Medal 2015.

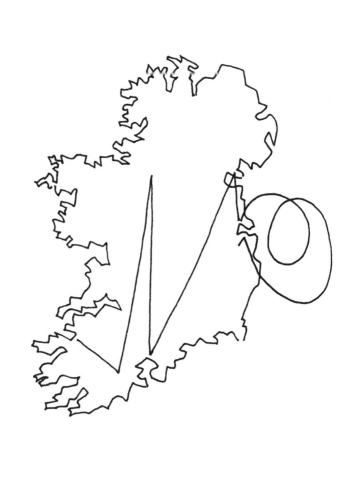